Violation of Trust

Whatever Happened to the Social Security Trust Funds?

by Steven J. Allen

Introduction by Jake Hansen,
Vice President for Government Affairs,
The Seniors Coalition

Foreword by Dr. Robert J. Myers
Former Deputy Commissioner
Social Security Administration

Violation of Trust:
Whatever Happened to the Social Security
Trust Funds?

First Edition
Library of Congress Catalog Card Number: 95-074711
ISBN 0-9648635-0-2

© 1995 The Seniors Coalition

Cover art by Artech
Book design by RR Research & Communications

Published by The Seniors Coalition
            11166 Main Street, Suite 302
            Fairfax, Virginia 22030

Published in the United States of America

INTRODUCTION

by Jake Hansen
Vice President for Government Affairs
The Seniors Coalition

Washington's handling of the Social Security trust funds is perhaps the most serious threat to the great social compact that links one generation to the next. This scandal, hidden from the public for years, can no longer be contained. This book comes at a time of great change in American politics and at a time of growing national awareness of the difficulties facing Social Security.

Before I go any farther, I want to acknowledge that this book could not have been possible without the help of Robert J. Myers. As a young man, Bob helped design the Social Security system and has dedicated his life to it ever since.

Bob is fond of saying that everyone has the right to their own opinions, but not their own facts. We are very fortunate to have been able to call on a person whom Senator Daniel Patrick Moynihan refers to as "a national treasure" to make certain our facts are accurate. I am proud to count Bob as a friend and an invaluable advisor to The Seniors Coalition.

Thanks go to the author, Steven J. Allen. Steve's background gives him a unique perspective on the problems facing Social Security in particular and the federal government in general. He is a lawyer, political scientist, and investigative reporter rolled into one, and he has worked on senior citizens' issues for nearly 15 years.

In 1995, we celebrated the 60th anniversary of Social Security. Looking back, Americans can take great pride in a benefits system that has helped so many people. But this year, and in the years to follow, we must fully realize that we face the difficult challenge of ensuring Social Security's continued survival. Unless action is taken, the Social Security Board of Trustees warns us, the system's Old-Age and Survivors Insurance (OASI) Trust Fund will soon face financial strains and will be completely broke in the year 2031. The Disability Insurance (DI) Trust Fund is projected to be exhausted in 2016. Although those dates sound like the distant future, the strains and political consequences are already being felt.

Of course, changes can be made to avert disaster, but The Seniors Coalition's experience has shown that restoring Social Security's financial integrity has never been a simple process. Members of The Seniors Coalition have been at the forefront of those efforts since the organization's inception in 1989.

The Seniors Coalition led the charge to roll back the Social Security earnings test, a rule that unfairly penalizes seniors who want to remain productive members of our work force. Members have successfully pushed for removing Social Security from the Department of Health and Human Services in order to make it an independent government agency. Members who have paid into Social Security throughout their working years have also successfully resisted efforts to subject benefits to means-testing. The Seniors Coalition has urged that Social Security be restored to an honest, pay-as-you-go system, advocated in favor of a balanced budget amendment to restore the system's integrity and have fought to remove the unfair tax on Social Security benefits signed into law by President Clinton in 1993.

Members of The Seniors Coalition can take

great pride that their organization was the first to sound the warning regarding Congress's use of the Social Security trust funds. As this book confirms, Americans have reason to be concerned about these questionable practices. Is our mammoth Social Security program backed by solid government trust fund bonds, or is it resting on a foundation of worthless IOUs? Americans are asking that very question with increasing frequency. If public confidence in Social Security is shattered, the system cannot survive. The government can no longer sweep questions about the trust funds under a carpet. If Social Security is to survive us, we must force our government officials to acknowledge the problem and correct it in the light of day.

It is my hope that this book will have a positive, educational impact on America's senior citizens and on Congress and the Administration. I hope that after you have read it, you will be motivated to make your voice heard as an advocate for reforming the Social Security trust funds and the treatment of their operations in the general budget.

FOREWORD

by Dr. Robert J. Myers
Former Deputy Commissioner
Social Security Administration

Don't panic!

The concerns expressed in this book are serious. But I am confident that the American people and our political leaders will deal with them in plenty of time to prevent any collapse of the Social Security system.

Since going to work on the Social Security program in 1934 for the organization that made the studies underlying it, housed in a few rooms down the street from the White House and called the

Committee on Economic Security, I have seen the critics come and go. Right now they are back, and polls indicate that public confidence in the system is weak, especially among young workers.

If you look just at the estimates of the actuaries, whose job it is to predict the financial futures of insurance and pension funds, then Social Security as it is now constituted is headed for a cliff. But that's only part of the story. It doesn't take into account human nature and political reality. And it doesn't take into account that the program can be changed — as it has at many times in the past.

For 23 years I served as Social Security's chief actuary. I learned that actuarial estimates sort of fire a shotgun at the future, and the truth often lies somewhere around the middle of the pattern. These middle-of-road forecasts may be too optimistic or too pessimistic, but they're as good as any.

Current figures for the program as it now exists show that, into the next century, Social Security will have income well in excess of outgo. According to some people, the first signs of financial trouble show up in the year 2013. The amount of money coming in from taxes in that year will equal the money being paid out in administrative costs and benefits: $986 billion. However, as in previous years, interest on the trust fund investments is also available to meet the outgo.

By the year 2019, annual spending on benefits will be a record $1.52 trillion. Nevertheless, the assets of the Social Security trust funds will reach the highest level in history: $3.31 trillion.

By the year 2020, the money coming in from taxes and interest won't be enough to pay the benefits, and Social Security will have to start selling its bonds to meet the outgo. That will be the beginning of the end under this scenario that present provisions of law will not change. A trust fund that took more than 80 years to build up will decrease so rapidly that it will disappear in just 10 years, by early 2030.

This is what doomsday would look like under this scenario. But none of us is ever going to see it. Some 81 million retirees, their dependents, and survivors will be drawing benefits from Social Security in the year it's supposed to go broke. Having them go from a check one month to nothing the next is unthinkable. The country wouldn't stand for it.

But if Social Security is unassailable politically, why is there so much worry about its future? Why is it true, as a recent poll suggests, that more young people say that they believe in flying saucers than have confidence that Social Security will be there for them when they retire? Or, with respect to the flying saucers, are they just answering a dumb question with a silly answer?

I believe that the problem of public confidence is largely the result of the system's current "roller-coaster" financing, in which a huge trust fund balance is built up and then goes downhill rapidly until it is exhausted.

A huge balance isn't necessary, however. In a private plan, it is necessary to build up reserves because of the possibility that the employer might go out of business. This gives some guarantee to participants and pensioners that the promised benefits will be paid. In a national program such as Social Security, this is not necessary. It is reasonably assumed that the national government will last forever.

This is an argument for "pay-as-you-go" financing, which is the way the system was funded in the 1960s and early 1970s.

Under such a financing system, the trust fund balance would equal only the approximate amount that will have to be paid out in benefits and administrative expenses in the next year. This would cushion the system against economic shocks and give breathing room to political leaders who might have to step in sometime in the future to make some adjustments. It would maintain the system on a constantly solid footing, instead of the current approach that either has the program awash in money or falling into the abyss.

As you read this book, keep in mind that — all in all — the Social Security system has worked. The American people can be secure in the knowledge that it will outlive us all.

———

Dr. Robert J. Myers, one of the architects of the Social Security system, is Chairman of the Board of Advisors of The Seniors Coalition. He was Chief Actuary of the Social Security Administration during 1947-70, Deputy Commissioner of Social Security in 1981-82, and Executive Director of the National Commission on Social Security Reform in 1982-83.

1.

PROVEN RIGHT

The misuse of the Social Security trust funds was supposed to be kept under wraps. For years, many who tried to expose it were accused of lying — and worse.

Two scenes, separated by three years:

SCENE ONE: *Room B-318, the Rayburn House Office Building in the U.S. Capitol complex, Thursday, May 14, 1992, 10:30 a.m.*

At a joint hearing of two Congressional subcommittees, one official after another called for dramatic action against an insidious menace. Evil people, it was suggested, were frightening America's senior citizens about the financial condition of Social Security.

Congressman Andy Jacobs, chairman of the Social Security subcommittee of the House Ways and Means Committee, demanded fines and prison terms for the malefactors. Congressman Peter Visclosky called for the application of forfeiture laws, normally used against drug dealers, in order to seize the villains' personal assets. Gwendolyn King, commissioner of Social Security, declared that Congress and the White House had a responsibility to stop the "inhumanity" that was being perpetrated.

Soon, calls for censorship were coming from every direction — from the American Association of Retired Persons, from the Attorney General of the State of New York, from ABC News, from *The New York Times*. In an editorial, the *Times* suggested that "The I.R.S. could . . . require mailings to be submitted for inspection" in order to stop letters that "scare [senior citizens] half to death."

What was the message so dangerous that top government officials and *The New York Times* demanded it be censored?

• That the Social Security trust funds are used to mask the size of the true deficit,

• That, because the government "lends" to itself, part of the trust fund money is used to finance day-to-day operations of the federal government, and

• That the only thing protecting the future Social Security benefits of American workers and retirees is their ability to organize and communicate with their elected officials.

SCENE TWO: *The Office of the Speaker, U.S. House of Representatives, U.S. Capitol, 8 p.m., Friday, April 7, 1995.*

In a nationally televised address, Speaker Newt Gingrich marked the completion of the "Contract with America."

The Contract was the platform on which Republicans won their first House majority in four decades. It included a specific list of legislative proposals, but more than anything else the Contract was a promise to the American people to change the way Washington works. In one way at least, Gingrich kept that promise; he spoke honestly about the problem of the Social Security trust funds.

"In fact," Gingrich said, "the money the government supposedly has been putting aside from the baby boomers' Social Security taxes is not there. The government has been borrowing that money to pay for the budget deficit. The Social Security Trust Fund is simply IOUs from the U.S. Treasury. So when the baby boomers get set to retire, where's the money going to come from? Well, you might ask, can't the federal government just borrow more money? The honest answer is no. No system, no country is wealthy enough to have unlimited borrowing."

Social Security, Gingrich said, "would be fine *if the government would stop borrowing the money.*"

There were those who disagreed with elements of Gingrich's statement; the objections of Dr. Robert J. Myers are noted elsewhere in this book. But the fact is that Gingrich's speech, along with similar declarations by Clinton Administration officials and by leading journalists and economists, brought vindication for those who had sounded an alarm about the trust funds.

———

The Seniors Coalition was, in fact, the first seniors' organization to blow the whistle. Over the past few years, the organization distributed tens of millions of newspapers, brochures, books, and informational letters alerting seniors to the trust fund problem.

As a consequence, some people in politics and the news media attacked The Seniors Coalition without mercy. TSC was accused of "fear-mongering" and of sending "fright mail" to seniors.

Powerful men in Congress called on authorities such as the U.S. Postal Inspector and state attorneys general to investigate TSC and the "misleading" information it was putting out as part of a "scam" to cheat seniors.

What a difference three years can make, between "Scene One" in 1992 and "Scene Two" in 1995!

Today, the trust fund problem is acknowledged by Democrats, Republicans, and independents across the political spectrum. [See the appendix to this book.] The Seniors Coalition has been proven right. In the view of many public officials and media pundits, including former critics, TSC has won tremendous credibility for having stood its ground — for having told the truth in the face of smears and threats.

But questions remain about what has been called the "raid" on the Social Security trust funds.

Is it a mere blunder by politicians with little understanding of economics? Is it an inevitable, though unintended, result of efforts to use taxpayers' money to buy votes? Is it a swindle?

In this book, we'll try to answer those questions.

———

If you're like most Americans, you have paid year after year into the Social Security system. As a law-abiding, taxpaying citizen, you have "contributed" an amount that seems like a king's ransom. Your employer has "contributed" a like amount, probably reducing the wages you would otherwise receive, so in reality you've paid for Social Security not once but twice.

In return, all you ask is that the government keep its promises. All you want is to get the benefits to which you are entitled.

Is that too much to ask? Is it unreasonable to expect that the government should keep its word to America's senior citizens — those who have spent their lives dutifully paying taxes, obeying the law, fighting to protect our country's freedom, and working hard to build the nation's economy?

Seniors have paid their dues. They deserve (among other things) the Social Security benefits they have earned.

Unfortunately, some politicians want to continue to use the Social Security trust funds to hide the real budget deficit, thus freeing them to spend more money on pork-barrel projects and other special interest spending. They want to use Social Security as an excuse to raise taxes on working people and small business people.

In old Western movies, the good guys wear

white hats and the bad guys wear black hats. Telling the good guys from the bad guys in Washington is not so easy.

The big spenders who use the trust funds to mask the deficit often masquerade as friends of senior citizens. Actually, they seek more power for themselves and for their friends and cronies.

Cynics say that, to hold onto public office with all its perks and privileges, the typical Washington "insider" would sell out his own grandmother. Come to think of it — when they mess with Social Security, that's exactly what they're doing.

There are some heroes, though, even in Washington. There are a few hardy souls in public office who really care about the people they represent, who fight for what is right, regardless of the consequences to themselves. These heroes need and deserve our support.

As for the other kind of politician... well, it's time seniors rose up in a ballot-box rebellion against them. It's time Americans joined together to send the message that we are fed up with tax-and-spend-and-waste, and we won't take it any more.

It's said there are two kinds of people: those who work for a living and those who vote for a living. The federal government spends too much time and effort protecting the special interests of people who vote for a living, and not enough time and effort protecting ̲̲̲̲̲̲ ̲̲̲̲ ̲̲ike us who have worked hard year after y̲̲̲r to provide for ourselves and our children.

The Social Security system is not perfect — no system is — but it represents a solemn promise made to each of us by our government. It represents a promise that must be kept.

The first step to changing our government's direction is for us to learn everything we can about the political system, how it works and how it fails to protect our interests.

In this book, we'll tell you a little about the history and purposes of Social Security. We'll explain how the politicians "borrowed" the Social Security money and used it to pay for everything from battleships to paper clips. We'll describe how the trust fund investment procedure set the stage for the biggest spending binge in American history.

When you're finished reading this book, you may be upset, and you may be angry. But you may also be inspired to fight for the future that hard-working, taxpaying Americans have earned.

And you'll realize that, by working to preserve and defend Social Security, you're not just helping senior citizens. You're also helping all the senior citizens of tomorrow.

2.
THE ORIGIN OF SOCIAL SECURITY

Social Security is tailored to fit the needs of Americans. It is not just given to people; it is <u>earned</u>. But, from the very beginning, its creators were concerned that politicians wouldn't be able to keep their hands off the money.

Social Security is a masterpiece of policy-making. From the beginning of the New Deal, it was a top priority at the Labor Department; but once FDR gave a clear go-ahead, it was developed by a committee in seven months, then pushed through Congress in another seven months. It has survived for six decades.

Yet the specific design of Social Security is a result of historical accidents, of political compromises made in the uncooled heat of a Washington summer. A slight change in the course of events and Social Security would be a very different system from the one we know today; a slight shift in the opposite direction and it wouldn't exist at all. An earlier vote in a key committee would have killed it. Social Security as we know it might never have been proposed if the Kingfish had been shot earlier, or if a country doctor hadn't noticed three women going through the garbage. But we're getting ahead of the story...

———

In the pre-industrial world, all but a tiny minority lived in what would today be considered abject poverty. As the Industrial Revolution brought newfound wealth (and much longer life expectancy) to hundreds of millions of people, there arose divisions between the growing ranks of the wealthy and middle class and those who were less well off.

In 1887, Edward Bellamy's book *Looking Backward* promised a science-fictional utopia of a future in which the government would take care of people "from cradle to grave" (the first known use of that term). It was only the second work of American literature to sell a million copies. Like the first million-copy book — *Uncle Tom's Cabin*, which fired the abolitionist movement —

Looking Backward was highly influential on American intellectuals. Eleanor Roosevelt, for example, was a big fan.

Meanwhile, U.S. courts began to eliminate one by one the restrictions the Constitution had previously placed on government intervention in the economy. As the 19th Century ended and the 20th Century began, the time was ripe for experimentation in the use of government power to help the less fortunate.

Senior citizens were to be among the first groups that governments would try to help. In those days, most seniors continued to work, if they were able, long past what would later be considered retirement age. Older people usually lived with their children or grandchildren or other relatives. Most had saved during their working lives to provide for their later years.

But what about seniors who were too sick to continue working? What about those who did not have relatives willing or able to take them in? What about those whose savings had been wiped out by natural or economic disaster? They depended on private charity, as did about seven percent of elderly Americans in 1929.

People asked: Can't a relatively wealthy society provide them with some sort of pension, to supplement what they could provide for themselves?

Most historians trace the origin of Social Security to the program of Otto von Bismarck, Imperial Germany's so-called Iron Chancellor. Socialists were organizing in Germany and most other Western countries, and Bismarck sought to weaken the socialists' political appeal. Beginning in 1881, he instituted a social insurance program. By 1889, it included government pensions for people age 70 or older. In the 1910s, the pension program was extended to cover disabled persons and those age 65-69.

In Great Britain, the Old Age Pensions Act of 1908 granted a weekly pension to any person over the age of 70 whose income fell below a certain level; the amount varied depending on income. There was no requirement for "contributions"; the pensions were paid out of general tax revenues. What set the law apart from earlier Poor Laws was the fact that the pension was regarded as a right whose receipt, in the words of the act, "shall not deprive the pensioner of any franchise, right or privilege, or subject him to any disability." In other words, accepting the pension did not cost you your right to vote.

Poland followed with a social insurance system in 1911, Holland and Sweden in 1913.

The British and Swedish systems were of special interest to the New Dealers. Sweden's system, which required "contributions," paid a pension to all persons age 67 or older. The size of the payments was based on the amount each individual had paid into the system, supplemented by government funds.

Spain instituted a social insurance system in 1919 and France in 1928. A total of 22 European and six non-European countries had social insurance programs by the mid-1930s.

Even in the United States, the idea of government pensions for seniors was not new. Many men and their widows were covered by Civil War pensions. The federal government had a huge surplus; the Republican platform of 1888 pledged support for veterans and their widows because, "In the presence of an overflowing treasury, it would be a public scandal to do less for those whose valorous service preserved the government." By 1893, 41.5 percent of the federal budget went to the pensions. Even in 1910, 45 years after the war, 28.5 percent of elderly men and eight percent of elderly women were covered. But the beneficiaries were dying out, and the system of Civil War pensions was vanishing — much to the frustration of reformers who wanted the system expanded into a broader system of social insurance.

The Populist Party of the 1890s and the Progressive movement promoted the idea of social insurance. When former President Teddy Roosevelt ran for the White House as a third-party candidate in 1912, his platform included the idea. Between 1910 and 1915, America's business establishment, through organizations such as the American Association for Labor Legislation, began a major push for social insurance.

In the United States, the Alaska territory in 1915 became the first government to enact an old-age assistance plan — though as late as 1934 it had fewer than 500 beneficiaries.

In 1921, the social insurance campaign was joined by a middle-class grassroots organization, the Fraternal Order of Eagles (FOE). The American Association for Old Age Security was founded by Abraham Epstein, a former lobbyist for FOE who believed that FOE was too willing to compromise. Epstein's group later became the American Association for Social Security.

Montana in 1923 was the first state with an old-age pension law. In 1930, New York Governor Franklin D. Roosevelt signed legislation providing for aid to poor senior citizens. Wisconsin adopted unemployment insurance in 1932. By the mid-'30s there were social assistance programs in 28 states, though most old-age pensions were low, and most old-age assistance programs excluded seniors who had children or grandchildren able to support them financially.

———

The social insurance movement would no doubt have had a major impact on U.S. and world politics even if the economic situation had been stable. But, as we have noted, the United States was a highly individualistic country that would probably have resisted that trend, had it not been for the near-total collapse of the economy.

In the late 1920s, the federal government (through the Federal Reserve System) caused a decline in the amount of money relative to the supply of goods and services. Prices fell by almost a quarter between 1929 and 1933, and many debtors were pushed over the edge into financial ruin. (Just as unanticipated inflation favors debtors, who can pay their debts back in cheaper dollars, unanticipated deflation favors creditors. A person who borrowed enough money to buy a modest home might have to pay back the price of a mansion.) Meanwhile, the federal government put high tariffs on foreign goods, which ruined foreign trade by depriving other countries of the dollars they needed to buy American goods.

The result was the Great Depression.

As the stock market crashed and as banks failed, millions of people saw their savings wiped out. People wanted the government to do something — anything — to provide relief. People's faith in their economic and political system was shaken. From the lowest-paid laborer to the highest-paid corporate president, Americans were scared and desperate. Communism, national socialism (Nazism), the democratic socialism of Norman Thomas, and other extreme political ideologies attracted millions of followers. To many people, the idea that the United States might become a totalitarian dictatorship as Russia was, and as Germany would soon become, was not so farfetched in those days. People, especially seniors whose life savings had been wiped out, were clutching at straws.

Franklin Delano Roosevelt, elected in 1932 on a platform of cutting government spending and balancing the budget, was both an able politician with an eye on the next election and a compassionate man who wanted to save his countrymen from the twin threats of privation and dictatorship.

In the creation of a social insurance system, FDR's political and patriotic interests came together.

The Socialist Party in 1928 and 1932 had called in its platform for "A system of . . . old-age pensions." The Socialists got nearly 900,000 votes in the 1932 election, and Roosevelt wanted those votes in the Democratic column.

In 1933, the Rockefeller Foundation brought two Englishmen, Sir William Beveridge and Sir Henry Steel-Maitland, to the U.S. to meet with business leaders and church organizations and speak to Rotary Clubs. Their job was to persuade American leaders that the British social security program worked fine. According to FDR's secretary of labor, Frances Perkins, they "did a great deal to allay the fears and doubts of the business and conservative part of the community." Beveridge would meet with FDR in 1934. That year, the President signed the Railroad Retirement Act, which covered railroad workers and was a precursor to Social Security.

A movement strikingly similar to the Ross Perot movement of the 1990s was sweeping the country in the mid-'30s. It began, according to the oft-told story, when a 66-year-old country doctor from Long Beach, California, named Francis Everett Townsend looked out his window while shaving and saw three "haggard" elderly women scrounging for food in garbage cans, "stooped with great age, bending over the barrels, clawing into the contents."

He wrote a letter to a newspaper (*The Long*

Beach Press-Telegram, September 30, 1933) about his plan for an "Old Age Revolving Pension" and became immensely popular, with millions of followers and a movement — the Townsendites — that lasted into the 1940s.

Townsend's plan was to give every person age 60 or older (other than convicted criminals) a $150-a-month pension — he would soon raise the figure to $200 a month — on the conditions that the beneficiary would not work and would spend the money in the United States within 30 days. The plan was to be financed by a two percent transactions tax similar to a sales tax; today we would call it a Value Added Tax or VAT. Financial experts proclaimed that the revenue from the two percent tax would be far short of the amount needed to finance the pensions.

At the time Townsend proposed a $200-a-month pension for each senior — a $400-a-month pension for a couple — an average worker made $100 a month. Only 13 percent of American families had incomes of $200 a month or more.

Although, as one of the architects of Social Security, J. Douglas Brown, has pointed out, the Townsend plan was "dangerous and illusory," it nevertheless "showed how scared the old people were."

On January 1, 1934, Townsend and an associate incorporated Old Age Revolving Pensions, Inc., known as OARP. By the end of 1934, there were more than a thousand Townsend Clubs across the country; *Time* magazine in January 1935 reported that there were perhaps 25,000 clubs with a total membership of perhaps four million. A national weekly publication was launched. In 1934, Townsendites claimed to have captured the legislatures of seven states.

As the Townsend movement roared across the country, the crusading writer Upton Sinclair, an avowed Socialist, won the 1934 Democratic nomination for governor of California on the "EPIC" platform — "End Poverty in California." He had written in his 1933 book *The Way Out* that government economic planning would lead to utopia, that "in a cooperative society every man, woman, and child would have the equivalent of $5,000 a year income from labor of the able-bodied young men for three or four hours per day." Sinclair lost the general election, but only after his Republican opponent endorsed the Townsend plan.

Meanwhile, Huey Long, the firebrand Senator from Louisiana known as "The Kingfish," proposed a "Share Our Wealth" program guaranteeing every person a $5,000 annual income, a homestead, free college education, and a pension for needy persons over age 60. This was to be financed by a tax on wealth ranging up to 99 percent on an "eight-millionaire," someone with an income of $8 million or more.

Long, who unveiled his plan in a nationwide radio address in 1934 and even wrote a song to go with his program ("Every Man a King!"), was a major rival of FDR. "I remember when he just scared the dickens out of Mr. Roosevelt and went on a nationwide radio hookup talking for old folks' pensions. And out of this probably came our Social Security system," said Long's son Russell, who was later a powerful U.S. Senator.

Polls at the time indicated that Long's entry into the 1936 presidential race as an independent could split the Democratic vote and throw the election to the Republicans. But Long was assassinated in Baton Rouge in September 1935, a few weeks after he filibustered to tie up funds for the new Social Security Board.

Long's son, Senator Russell Long, later pointed out that "My father was calling for a social security program long before President Roosevelt proposed one. In fact, when Roosevelt presented his social security program, he was advocating it as an alternative to what Huey Long was proposing."

An unemployment insurance bill had been introduced in Congress in 1933, but, as Frances

Perkins later wrote, "there was a great demand for old age insurance also. It was easy to add this feature — and politically almost essential. One hardly realizes nowadays how strong was the sentiment in favor of the Townsend Plan and other exotic schemes for giving the aged a weekly income. In some districts the Townsend Plan was the chief political issue, and men supporting it were elected to Congress. The pressure from its advocates was intense. The President began telling people he was in favor of adding old-age insurance clauses to the bill and putting it through as one program."

Roosevelt was more concerned with the right-now than the down-the-road.

"Fear and worry based on unknown danger contribute to social unrest and economic demoralization," he told Congress in a June 8, 1934, address. "If, as our Constitution tells us, our federal government was established among other things 'to promote the general welfare,' it is our plain duty to provide for that security upon which welfare depends."

So, on June 29, 1934, FDR formed a Cabinet-level group, the Committee on Economic Security. Its chairman was Labor Secretary Frances Perkins, the first woman to serve in a President's Cabinet. She had served under Roosevelt in New

York's state government, and she had agreed to become secretary of labor only on the condition that Roosevelt was to propose both unemploy-ment-compensation and old-age pensions.

The technical staff of the Committee was mostly from Wisconsin, a place that epitomized "progres-sivism" in the sense that Berkeley, California, does today. The committee brought together leading experts to draft plans for unemployment compen-sation laws, welfare, and old-age pensions.

J. Douglas Brown, a member of the task force that drew up the Social Security proposal, said the group looked at European models of national pen-sion plans, including the English system that of-fered a flat sum for each retiree. But, to empha-size individual responsibility, the group designed a plan in which "you get what you pay for" and ben-efits were based on the wage earned and length of employment. Brown said the idea was "Every-body pays for their own ticket" — each person *earns* a pension, rather than having one handed to him or her. (He obviously did not mean that each person gets back exactly what he or she paid in.)

Frank Bane, the first chief administrative of-ficer of Social Security, said in 1983 that even FDR himself had concerns: "Roosevelt ran more or less as a conservative, but he was scared to death by the Townsend plan . . ." John Gunther, in *Roosevelt in Retrospect* (1950), wrote that "Some of his own advisers wanted him to support the Townsend Plan for old-age pensions; it might have brought him millions of votes. He would have none of it, and worked out instead the more moderate, sensible, and humane social security statute that is in force today."

As designed by the task force, Social Security was meant as an alternative to unearned, means-tested benefits; it was supposed to help people who worked hard and paid their taxes, not people who were lazy and irresponsible. The idea was that Social Security (including unemployment insurance) would help make the dole (welfare) obsolete.

Thomas Eliot, who drafted the Social Security bill, said FDR vetoed the idea of using general tax revenues to finance the program. "We must not have a dole — even in the future," Roosevelt reportedly said.

Wilbur Cohen, who started work on Social Security as a 21-year-old fresh out of the University of Wisconsin and went on to be secretary of Health, Education, and Welfare, remarked years later that Roosevelt insisted on funding the program through payroll taxes because "financing the program by earmarked payroll taxes would ensure that a future President and Congress could not, morally or politically, repeal or mutilate the 'entitlement character of the program.'"

Explaining Social Security in the 1936 book *Forward with Roosevelt*, P.J.O'Brien wrote: "Every worker, except certain exempt classes, and those who have reached the age of sixty-five years, will come under the act regardless of whether he has a million in the bank or is behind in his instalments [sic] on his third-hand automobile. So will the girl who chooses to work after she gets married."

The universal aspect of Social Security — that it went to everyone who qualified, and that no "means test" would penalize people for saving and investing — was the cornerstone of the program.

———

Some elements of Social Security were essential. Some were arbitrary.

The retirement age was set at 65 for several reasons. The retirement age under the original Social Security system, in Bismarck's Germany, was 70, later lowered to 65. Most states with old-age pensions set the age at 65 or 70. The Townsend Plan set the age at 60. Sixty-five seemed to be a reasonable compromise. Besides, the numbers added up. Sixty-five was the youngest retirement age that seemed economically feasible.

Dr. Robert J. Myers, former chief actuary and deputy commissioner of Social Security, wrote in his book *Within the System*: "In 1934 we figured that men who were 65 years old could, on the average, expect to live another 12 years. For women it was 13 years. The bottom line was that we figured it would cost $22 billion in the aggregate to give a $25 monthly pension for life. And that was a lot of money in those days.

"Now here's the arbitrary part. Age 65 was picked because 60 was too young and 70 was too old. So we split the difference," Myers wrote.

Of course, that choice didn't satisfy everyone. The state of medical science and the attitudes of the day were reflected in the comments of Congressman Henry Ellenbogen of Pennsylvania: "The 65-year limit in the [Social Security] bill must go. It is entirely too high. After all, this is supposed to be a pension for old age, not a graveyard pension. Most people who are 60 years of age are old; the years ahead of them hold no prospect of jobs or gainful occupation. They have every right to live their last years in comfort, in economic peace and security."

Social Security wasn't just benefits for retired workers. In fact, the retirement program was originally only "a minor part" of the program, Wilbur Cohen said later.

The Social Security Act would establish the Aid to Dependent Children program, which was renamed Aid to Families with Dependent Children in 1962 and today is the principal program among the hundreds known collectively as "welfare."

Another part of the Social Security Act would establish a system of unemployment insurance. It did not create a federal system but indirectly forced states to do so. A federal tax was imposed on payrolls, but an employer could deduct most of the payments from federal taxation if the business was covered by a state unemployment insurance program. Employers in states without unemployment insurance laws had to pay the full federal tax, so states quickly enacted such laws.

Originally there was supposed to be a health care component to Social Security, but it was dropped out of fear that the provision would bring the whole program down to defeat.

The unemployment-compensation and welfare parts of the Social Security Act were to be administered by the states. So was the part of the plan designed to benefit people who were needy and had already reached retirement age; grants-in-aid would go to the states for payments to the elderly poor.

But the old-age insurance part — the part that people usually mean today when they refer to Social Security — was to be administered at the federal level.

The committee writing the Social Security legislation was careful to draw the plan so that it could be upheld by the Supreme Court. Thomas Eliot noted, "You had a Supreme Court that was knocking down every New Deal law that it could get its hands on. . . . [In drafting the legislation] We put the two titles — one tax and one benefits — quite far apart and never called the old-age benefits 'insurance.' We were trying to capture a stray justice and give him a peg to hang his hat on."

Read that quote again. Eliot was noting that, in order to get Social Security past the Supreme Court, the drafters kept the tax part of the program separate from the benefits part. As far as the law was concerned, the taxes and benefits were unrelated items. That is an important point to remember, because if the taxes and benefits are separate items, the federal government is under no legal obligation to provide benefits in return for the taxes that have been paid.

In other words: Working Americans may have been promised Social Security benefits in exchange for tax "contributions," but they cannot enforce that promise in the courts if a future President and Congress change the program. Later in this book, we will examine what this means for current and future Social Security beneficiaries.

———

The Committee on Economic Security's report — written by Edwin Witte, a University of Wisconsin economics professor and the committee's executive director — was filed January 15, 1935. The White House made a few changes, such as the elimination of the likelihood of a large deficit after 1965 that would tap the federal government's general revenues. On January 17, a 65-page bill was sent to Congress.

The House Ways and Means Committee at first seemed unlikely to approve the measure — leaders told FDR that approval was impossible — but after a provision for the sale of individual old-age annuities was dropped, the committee voted on April 5 to approve Social Security. The vote was almost along party lines, with Republicans opposed and all but one Democrat in favor.

On the House floor, there were 50 amendments, all of which failed decisively.

Considering the speed with which Social Security moved through Congress, one might assume that old-age pensions were immensely popular. But, according to political analysts, it was the welfare and unemployment compensation parts of Social Security that were wildly popular in Depression-plagued America. Most political analysts believe the old-age benefits would not have been approved if they had not been part of a package with the welfare and unemployment compensation measures.

There were other bumps along the way toward passage. Individualistic Americans were afraid of anything that smacked of Big Government — Social Security numbers, for example. Rumors were rampant about how the numbers would be used. The Hearst newspapers caught wind of a proposal to issue everyone dog tags with their Social Security numbers on them. "Military regimentation" it was called. The dog tag rumor apparently originated with a company that wanted to produce metal nameplates for Social Security enrollees.

But instead of dog tags, cards were to be issued. To calm their anxiety regarding privacy, Americans were promised that the law would prohibit the use of Social Security numbers as identification. (The U.S. military has used them for identification since 1943, the Internal Revenue Service since 1961.)

Key to the passage of Social Security was the

support of Big Business, including officials of General Electric, Standard Oil, the Chase Manhattan Bank, U.S. Rubber, Procter and Gamble, Cannon Towels, Filene's, Mead Corporation, and the firms of Goldman, Sachs and Brown Brothers, Harriman.

After final approval in both houses, Roosevelt signed the act with old-fashioned wooden pens at about 3:30 p.m. on August 14, 1935. It was less than 14 months from the time the committee was appointed until the measure became law.

By 1936, the Social Security Board set up shop in Washington, with the records later being maintained in a Baltimore warehouse. The first district office was in Austin, Texas.

Collection of payroll taxes began in 1937 at a rate of two percent (combined employees' and employers' share) on the first $3,000 of wages. The maximum: $60 a year.

On May 24, 1937, the Supreme Court voted 7 to 2 that the Social Security old age program was constitutional. However, in a separate case on the unemployment insurance part of Social Security, the employers' payroll tax was upheld by a single vote, 5 to 4. A different outcome in that case might have brought down the entire system.

Even before the first monthly benefit checks went out, the Social Security plan was amended in

1939 to provide benefits for spouses and survivors and to advance the first date of payment from 1942 to 1940.

Ida Mae Fuller of Vermont was a legal secretary who, together with her employer, paid $44 into the system for three years before her retirement. On January 31, 1940, she got the first Social Security check, for $22.54. She lived another 35 years to age 100 and collected $20,884.52 in benefits. For some people Social Security wasn't just a good deal, it was a wonderful deal.

The first monthly checks went out in 1940. By the end of the year, there were 222,000 beneficiaries. Total benefits distributed: about $35 million that year.

Social Security was so well-designed that it seemed it could go on forever. It was nearly four decades before the system got into financial trouble (as we shall see in the next chapter).

3.

Changes

As time passed, politicians fiddled with the Social Security system. Coverage was extended and new benefits were added. But eventually the money began to run out.

By 1950, it was clear that current payroll tax revenues were always going to be used to provide for current recipients, on an approximate "pay-as-you-go" basis. Then coverage was extended to the vast majority of Americans, and benefits, which remained stable through the war and its aftermath, were increased an average of 77 percent, reflecting the increase in the cost of living.

In the 1950s, Social Security coverage was extended to groups not included in the original program: farm workers; domestic workers; self-employed people including lawyers and dentists; clergy and other employees of charitable, educational, and religious nonprofit organizations; some state and local government employees; and members of the armed forces.

(Members of the armed forces joined the Social Security program on a "contributory" basis in 1957. The federal government was supposed to allocate money to the Social Security trust funds to provide for benefits for members of the armed forces with regard to service before that year. But, as Senator Daniel Patrick Moynihan has noted, the government "forgot" to allocate this money — for over three decades.)

In 1954, the combined payroll tax reached four percent on the first $3,600. The maximum: $144 a year.

In 1956, Congress gave women the option to retire at age 62 with reduced benefits, a provision extended to men five years later.

Also in 1956, Congress established a cash benefit program for disabled workers age 50 or older. In 1958, dependents of disabled workers became eligible for benefits, and in 1960 the age requirement was dropped.

(As an example of how government programs expand, consider that these benefits for the disabled, as approved in 1956, were supposed to cost $860 million by 1980. Adjusted for inflation, the figure would have been $2.6 billion. But, largely because of the liberalization of benefits, the actual cost in 1980 was $16 billion.)

In 1960, the combined payroll tax for employers and employees reached six percent on the first $4,800. The maximum: $288 a year.

In 1965, Medicare was added to provide — first for persons age 65 and older, then for the long-term disabled — hospital insurance and the opportunity to purchase subsidized insurance for physician care.

Also in 1965, the Johnson Administration took a major step expanding Social Security. "Some of the biggest increases since the program began and a whopping hike in the minimum benefit came during the Great Society years, when President Johnson sought to increase the minimum benefit to help old poor people," wrote LBJ aide Joseph Califano. "To the protests that we were turning Social Security into a 'welfare program' unworthy of our senior citizens, Johnson pointed out that in 1965 more than five million of the 17 million Americans over 65 were struggling to survive below the poverty line, even though they had spent most of their lives working. We won most of what we asked for on Capitol Hill . . ."

In 1971, the combined employer/employee payroll tax reached 10.4 percent on the first $7,800. The maximum: $811 a year (including the hospital insurance portion of Medicare).

In 1972, Congress voted to hike benefits 20 percent, but another change would have far greater consequences down the line. Until that year, there was an important limitation on the size of the Social Security budget: increases had to be approved by Congress, subject to the President's veto. That year the system was changed. Facing re-election — an easy re-election, as it turned out — President Nixon asked Congress to index benefits so that they would rise automatically with inflation beginning in 1975.

Congress eagerly complied with the Nixon request, adding a 20 percent increase in payments to beneficiaries. Nixon opposed this increase, but after it passed over his opposition, little slips giving him credit for the idea were inserted with each Social Security check.

Indexing benefits to inflation had two effects. First, it made it difficult to predict how high benefits would be in the future; it created a segment of the budget that would grow year after year even if no deliberate action was taken.

Second, it neutralized the most powerful political force for fighting inflation — seniors.

Inflation occurs when the amount of money increases faster than the size of the economy. For example, if the government doubled the supply of money tomorrow, each dollar would soon be worth 50 cents. When government simply creates money to pay its debts, you see situations such as that in post-World War I Germany when it took a wheelbarrow full of money to buy a piece of candy. Price increases don't cause inflation; inflation, the reduction of the value of a dollar, causes price increases.

Historically, seniors have been the hardest-hit by inflation, because it destroys the value of savings. As long as Social Security benefit increases had to be voted on, seniors had a strong incentive to vote for Congressmen and other public officials who opposed inflation. But once Social Security was indexed, most organizations that claim to speak for seniors began to support big-spenders, whose policies would create inflation.

Indexation also had a direct effect on Social Security funds. In 1975, Social Security began paying out more than it was taking in.

In 1976, Jimmy Carter ran on a platform of opposing future payroll tax increases and he implied that he would roll back the increases scheduled for 1978 and 1981. "He also committed himself to restoring the financial integrity of the system, but he never had to face what it would cost in taxes to keep that commitment," wrote Carter's Health and Human Services Secretary Joseph Califano.

A large tax increase was approved in 1977 to ensure that the program would always be financially sound. Or so the politicians promised.

Another change that made Social Security slightly more costly was the 1977 *Goldfarb* decision of the U.S. Supreme Court. Until that time, husbands and surviving widowers seeking benefits had to prove their working wives had provided at least one-half their support, though there was no such requirement for wives and widows of working husbands. The Supreme Court ruled that the requirement violated the equal protection clause of the U.S. Constitution. The Court then took it upon itself to extend the benefits to the husbands and widowers, costing the system $500 million to $1 billion a year.

With the tax hike of 1977, the combined payroll tax in 1978 (including Medicare hospital insurance) reached 12.1 percent on the first $17,700. The maximum: $2,142 a year.

———

Jimmy Carter's 1977 Social Security tax hike — $227 billion in new taxes over nine years, at that time the largest tax increase in American history — was supposed to keep the Social Security system well-funded and protected until the year 2030. Carter said that, "without this legislation, the Social Security reserve funds would have begun to be bankrupt in just a year or two, by 1979. Now this legislation will guarantee that from 1980 to the year 2030, the Social Security funds will be sound."

During his debate with Ronald Reagan in 1980, Carter reiterated his position. He said that, "although there was a serious threat to the Social Security system and its integrity during the 1976 campaign and when I became President, the action of the Democratic Congress working with me has been to put Social Security back on a sound financial basis. That's the way it will stay."

President Carter may have believed his statement was true, but it was not. His own administration was reporting at the time that tax hikes would be necessary to save the Social Security system. It was not secure until the year 2030; some experts estimated that it would go bust as early as 1983.

"Alas," columnist Doug Bandow wrote, "the year 2030 came along some 47 years early."

———

In the late 1970s, taxes and regulation were taking their toll on the economy. Inflation reached double digits, interest rates skyrocketed and real wages fell while unemployment increased. Meanwhile, the number of people covered by Social Security increased. By 1980, about 95 percent of the workforce was covered and benefits went to about 91 percent of the over-65 population, plus five million disabled people (workers, widows, and adult children) and their eligible dependents, and four million under-65 survivors. It was more of a strain on the system than most people realized. The system would be broke by 1983 unless something was done.

Social Security faced a danger that the over-used word "crisis" does not begin to convey. The money was running out. According to the official projections, the Social Security retirement and survivors' fund would be losing $47 million a day and by 1989 it would be losing between $104 million and $153 million a day.

The politicians said the system could never go broke, but some of the top experts on Social Security — people not inclined toward paranoia or fearmongering — were deeply concerned. In December 1981, President Reagan and Congressional leaders appointed a bipartisan commission, with eight Republican members and seven Democrats, to work out a plan to save the system again. Officially known as the National Commission on Social Security Reform, it was generally known as the Greenspan Commission, after its chairman Alan Greenspan.

It was the first time such a commission was appointed to deal with problems in the Social Security system, although there had been periodic advisory councils that were bipartisan.

As 1982 came to a close, it appeared that the commission might fail. Later, Dr. Robert J. Myers, the commission's executive director, described the mood among those working to save Social Security:

"There was deep gloom in the winter air. The fact still remained that somebody had to do something, and Congress would have to do something. Otherwise, come the middle of 1983, the fund balance would be down to zero, and the checks weren't going to go out on time. Thirty-six million people were looking for that government envelope in their mail at the first of every month.

"There wasn't going to be anything gradual about this. Social Security had to have the money to send out all of the checks, or it couldn't send out any of them."

The original December 31, 1982, deadline for the commission's recommendation came and went. Reagan had extended the commission's life to January 15, 1983. Finally, members came to agreement: a combination of tax hikes, a future phased-in increase in the retirement age from 65 to 67, an expansion of Social Security coverage to people who had previously been exempt, and cuts in future benefits (by skipping six months of the Cost of Living Adjustment). The proposal included the taxation of a portion of Social Security benefits; income taxes would apply to up to 50 percent of benefits, to the extent that a beneficiary's income (including "tax-exempt" income and half of Social Security benefits) exceeded $25,000 for individuals and $32,000 for couples.

The 15 commission members had plenty to disagree on. Three conservatives voted against the final report, which was approved 12 to 3. It was the result of compromise; not a single commissioner supported every aspect of the final report. There were 11 dissenting opinions — objections to one aspect of the plan or another — and every commissioner signed at least one dissenting opinion.

The commission's chairman, Alan Greenspan, told CNN: "None of this is any good except the conclusion."

The commission's executive director — the

aforementioned Dr. Robert J. Myers — wrote that, "If the commission had failed altogether, it would have been entirely up to Congress to do something about the problem because by June or July, the checks would not have gone out on time." Myers speculated that Congress would have found "a way to borrow some money to keep the system afloat . . . It may sound funny, but it's not hard to imagine the riots that could come from a sudden shutdown of the Social Security system."

The deal that was written into legislation was signed by President Reagan in a Rose Garden ceremony in 1982. Those present included House Speaker Tip O'Neill, Rules Committee Chairman Claude Pepper, Senate Majority Leader Robert Dole, and a host of other Congressional leaders.

Social Security was saved — for a while, anyway — but the rescue was costly. The rescue plan included the first "give-back" of Social Security benefits. For the first time, Social Security benefits would be taxed.

———

In 1988, the combined payroll tax (including Medicare hospital insurance) hit 15.02 percent on the first $45,000 of earnings. The maximum: $6,759 a year.

In 1993, President Clinton proposed an increase

from 50 percent to 85 percent in the maximum portion of Social Security benefits that could be subject to income tax. The Seniors Coalition sent out millions of letters and publications containing information on the Clinton proposal, and angry senior citizens urged members of Congress to oppose it. The result was a partial victory for seniors: The 85 percent bracket was applied only to income above $34,000 for an individual or $44,000 for a couple (with "tax-exempt" income and half of Social Security benefits included for purposes of calculating income).

Meanwhile, the payroll tax that finances Social Security and Medicare hospital insurance continued to rise. Today, the combined employer/employee payroll tax rate is 15.3 percent on the first $61,200 of earnings, or $9,363.60 per year. But that is not the maximum tax, because the portion of the payroll tax that finances Medicare hospital insurance (2.9 percent combined rate) applies to all earnings.

———

In 1936, a government pamphlet titled "Security in Your Old Age" noted that Social Security taxes would begin at one percent on the employer and one percent on the employee on wages up to $3,000. It would increase gradually until, "beginning in 1949, twelve years from now, you and your employer will each pay 3 cents on each dollar you earn, up to $3,000 a year. That is the most you will ever pay."

A total of $180 a year in 1949 — the equivalent of about $1,100 in today's dollars — was "the most you will ever pay." Yet the current annual tax (not counting the Medicare portion) is as much as $7,588.80.

One lesson we should learn is that government programs are, by their very nature, flexible. When we read that a certain tax is "the most you will ever pay," or when the government tells us a particular program will last forever without changes, we should be careful not to rely too much on those statements — no matter how much they may seem like promises.

4.
WILL WORKERS GET
A RAW DEAL?

Some claim that Social Security recipients get back much more than they paid in. In fact, with the exception of people who retired long ago, working Americans get only a small return on their "investment" in Social Security.

The changes proposed by the Greenspan Commission kept the system going. One reason for that success was the spectacular economic growth of the '80s. A single recession later in the decade might have busted the system again, as Richard Foster, deputy chief actuary for Social Security, noted in a 1983 memorandum:

"If actual growth is more rapid in 1983, but

then restricted by another recession within the next few years, the trust funds could be in a worse financial position than indicated under the pessimistic assumptions. . . . Depletion of the . . . trust funds would be very likely under these conditions and could conceivably occur within a few years from now."

Because of the Greenspan Commission reforms and because of economic growth during "Reaganomics" — the longest period of continuous economic growth in the peacetime history of the United States — the trust funds not only remained solvent, they grew a surplus that was used to make the federal deficit seem smaller than it really was.

But the tax reduction that was the key to the success of Reaganomics did not last.

After a brief respite during the early years of the Reagan Administration, federal taxes resumed their upward climb. Every time working people took home a paycheck, they noted the amount that was taken out for taxes. And, because low-income workers paid little or no federal income taxes, three-quarters of American taxpayers paid more in Social Security taxes (counting the employers' share) in 1990 than they paid in federal income taxes. As a result, much worker resentment was directed at the payroll tax.

In 1990, Senator Robert Kasten of Wisconsin noted that, "From 1955 to 1988, the tax burden on Americans rose twice as fast as their income." In 1955, a median-income family of four paid federal taxes at the rate of nine percent. In 1970, that family paid 16 percent. In 1988, that family paid 24 percent of its income in federal taxes alone, not counting state and local taxes.

Those tax increases hurt the economy and, in conjunction with rapidly increasing domestic federal spending, helped cause massive deficits.

Martin Feldstein, later Reagan's economic adviser, wrote in 1975 that, "Because of the vast size of the social security program and its central role in the American system of financing retirement, it has major effects on all the significant dimensions of our economy."

As anyone who ever refinanced a mortgage is aware, a small change in the interest rate can have a dramatic impact due to compounding. The same principle is true with regard to taxes and regulations that lessen the rate of economic growth.

Because payroll taxes are offset by Social Security benefits, the drag on the economy in any one year is small. But, over time, as the effect is compounded, the taxes may have a significant effect.

Some conservative economists estimated that,

by 1991, national income had been reduced by an estimated 20 percent compared to what it would have been without that tax burden. Other experts such as Dr. Robert J. Myers call that estimate nonsense.

One side of the debate is represented by former Reagan aide Peter Ferrara, who noted in a Heritage Foundation study:

"The payroll tax is a tax on employment. Thus at the margin, the tax discourages employers from hiring workers and discourages workers from accepting jobs. . . . And because the payroll tax increases the general cost of U.S. labor, it reduces U.S. international competitiveness. Poor competitiveness means that American businesses lose sales to foreign firms and Americans lose jobs to foreign workers. The result: fewer jobs and reduced economic growth. And the higher the payroll tax, the greater the damage."

In 1990, Senator Kasten and Senator Daniel Patrick Moynihan of New York introduced legislation to reduce the Social Security tax rate by up to $600 for a working couple. The Moynihan-Kasten proposal would have ended the practice of using the temporary surplus in the Social Security trust funds to mask the true size of the federal budget deficit — a practice that Moynihan, drawing attention to the issue, called "thievery."

Moynihan and Kasten asked: Why should the Social Security tax go to hide the size of the overall deficit in the federal budget? Why should people with lower incomes pay a tax at a higher rate than wealthier people, when that tax is used to finance, through government bonds, the general activities of the federal government?

Said Moynihan, "If we [Democrats] can't get behind an issue like this, of principle, then I'm not sure who needs the Democratic Party."

Conservative groups such as the National Taxpayers Union, the Cato Institute, and the Heritage Foundation endorsed a cut in the Social Security tax. "How can you be against such a good idea?" asked Donald Leavens of the U.S. Chamber of Commerce. "It's populist, and it will do a lot for economic growth." The idea had the support of liberals such as columnist Michael Kinsley and radicals such as Robert Borosage, policy director for Jesse Jackson's 1988 campaign. As then-Senator Jim Sasser (D-Tennessee) put it, "this thing could sprout wings and become an irresistible political juggernaut that will thunder through the halls of Congress like a rolling locomotive."

Why did the measure fail? Because the big spenders who dominated Congress and their friends in the media could not give up that method of hiding the horrendous budget deficit.

In October 1990, President George Bush caved in to pressure from Congressional Democrats and agreed to a substantial tax hike, rather than the tax cut that Kasten and Moynihan proposed. By breaking his "Read my lips: No new taxes" pledge, he caused or worsened a recession and scuttled his own re-election campaign. Congressional leaders had promised to cut spending, but spending continued to increase dramatically. With hindsight, it is obvious that Washington took the wrong path.

———

Today's workers aren't the only ones who may get less than they expect. A common belief is that retirees get back all they and their employers paid in Social Security taxes, plus interest, within three or four years. Although that was true for some of the earliest people to retire on Social Security, it certainly isn't true today.

Dean Baker of the Economic Policy Institute noted in a letter to *The Washington Post*: "If a worker earned the average wage every year from 1949 to 1994, and retired with the average benefit, his accumulated taxes would pay his benefit for more than 16 years. This calculation assumes a 3 percent real interest rate on all accumulated taxes. Furthermore, since taxes have been higher in recent years than they were in the early 1950s, this ratio is increasing. A person re-tiring in 1999 will have accumulated enough earn-ings to support 21 years of benefits. A person retiring in 2004 will have accumulated enough earnings to support 26 years of benefits."

Dr. Robert J. Myers believes that Baker's esti-mate of 16 years for a "payback" is too high. Myers' calculation (including both employer's and employee's taxes) projects a payback in 12 years, and he questions the full inclusion of the employer's share.

Either way, it seems clear that workers do not get their money back (assuming any reasonable rate of interest) within a short period, and that the payback period for a new retiree gets longer each year.

Some people will continue to argue that retir-ees get a bonanza from Social Security, and there-fore it's fair to cut benefits. With each year that passes, the effective rate of return gets smaller and that argument gets weaker.

Besides, nothing is guaranteed to future Social Security beneficiaries. The system is, of necessity, flexible. No matter what you think you've been promised, the government can change the Social Security system any way it wants — as we shall see in the next chapter.

5.
IS SOCIAL SECURITY'S FUTURE GUARANTEED?

Surprise! The federal government is under no legal obligation to pay you the Social Security benefits it has promised. Only the political power of beneficiaries and their families protects Social Security.

It is often said that Social Security is backed by the full faith and credit of the United States government, and that people are guaranteed the benefits for which they have paid.

But the truth is that nothing guarantees your Social Security except the good faith of the Congress and the White House. Social Security can be altered — or, theoretically, abolished — at any time, and you have no legal recourse.

If you have an annuity from a private insurance company, you have a right to your payments under the contract law. (In "participating" policies, the payment amount can go up or down, but not below a prescribed minimum.) But there is no corresponding right under Social Security.

This is necessary under the U.S. Constitution, and is the case for all government benefit programs. This flexibility can be an advantage at times, because benefits can be increased as well as decreased.

The lack of a "right" to Social Security — a seeming flaw in the system — was quite deliberate. As Eduard A. Lopez, formerly senior legislative assistant to Senator Daniel Patrick Moynihan of New York, noted, "in the mid-1930s a conservative Supreme Court was dealing fatal blows to many New Deal programs on the ground that they exceeded Congress's commerce power. To save the Social Security Act from this fate, its drafters (on advice to Labor Secretary Frances Perkins from Justice Harlan Stone) carefully crafted a bill that relied squarely on Congress's powers to tax and spend for the general welfare. To avoid the appearance of a pension scheme, they neatly separated tax and spending provisions of the bill and made no references to contractual or earned rights to benefits."

As far as the law is concerned, the taxes paid into the system and the benefits paid out are separate programs. Accordingly, Lopez wrote, "the Court held in 1960 that a Social Security claimant's legal interest in benefits is not an accrued property right for due-process purposes because workers neither earn benefits nor establish entitlement to them through their contributions. Rather, workers pay taxes and eligible retirees get benefits. Period."

Peter Ferrara of the National Center for Policy Analysis wrote that, "Though a taxpayer may pay thousands of tax dollars into social security over the course of his working years and base all his financial plans on receipt of the promised social security benefits, he still does not have a legally enforceable, contractual entitlement to these benefits, as he would in a private insurance program. In the case of *Flemming v. Nestor* (1960), the Supreme Court held that the government has the power to renege on social security benefit promises despite the payment of past taxes in anticipation of such benefits by the disappointed beneficiary."

In the *Flemming* case, the Supreme Court held: "To engraft upon the social security system a concept of 'accrued property rights' would deprive it of the flexibility and boldness in adjustment to ever changing conditions which it demands."

Justice Hugo Black dissented from the ruling. He wrote:

"The Court consoles those whose insurance is taken away today, and others who may suffer the same fate in the future, by saying that a decision requiring the social security system to keep faith would deprive it of the flexibility and boldness in adjustment to ever changing conditions which it demands. People who pay premiums for insurance usually think they are paying for insurance, not for flexibility and boldness. I cannot believe that any private insurance company in America would be permitted to repudiate its matured contracts with its policy-holders who have regularly paid all their premiums in reliance upon the good faith of the company."

Justice Black wrote that the members of the Supreme Court majority "simply tell the contributors to this insurance fund that despite their own and their employer's payments, the Government, in paying the beneficiaries out of the fund, is merely giving them something for nothing and can stop doing so when it pleases."

Of course, social insurance is different from private insurance. Each has its own advantages and disadvantages. Problems arise when people confuse the two, and when their expectations are based on that confusion.

———

The *Flemming* case explains why some critics attacked the Social Security system as a sort of "Ponzi scheme." Ponzi was a turn-of-the-century Boston con artist who used a simple technique to cheat people out of their money. Here's how the scheme works: As money comes in from the new investors, it is used to pay off people who invested previously. The earlier investors then attest to the worthiness of the investment, and their testimonials are used to recruit new participants. Of course, at some point the cash flow slows and there isn't enough money coming in to fulfill the promises made to investors. That's when the con man skips town.

Seniors are concerned that, at some point, Uncle Sam will skip town — that is, the federal government will renege on its promise to pay seniors their Social Security benefits.

Whether you think this concern is justified depends on your view of the federal government. But, as recently as 1993, Social Security benefits were cut; Robert Rubin, who was then a Clinton economic adviser and is now secretary of the treasury, said the Clinton Administration's "increase in taxes on the top tier of Social Security recipients is really a benefit reduction."

(The Seniors Coalition, by the way, vigorously opposed the tax increase/benefit cut, but most seniors' groups such as the American Association of Retired Persons did nothing to fight it.)

The pressure for the government to reduce Social Security benefits will build and build, unless and until the government gets its overall spending under control. That's because the ratio of payroll-taxpayers to beneficiaries has changed.

When a program such as Social Security or a private pension plan begins, those paying into the system greatly outnumber those receiving benefits. Thus, there is no problem meeting the system's obligations. For example, as long as population increases two percent a year and wages per person increase two percent a year, there can be increases in total benefits paid out.

But what happens when the rate of population growth declines from two percent a year (the typical rate for the U.S.) to half-a-percent or less (the recent figure)? What happens when the rate of wage increases over inflation is cut from two percent (the historical figure) to 1.3 percent (the average for the past few decades)?

What happens is that the money paid in can no longer cover the increased burden on the fund.

So what can be done to protect Social Security funds? What can be done to protect it from politicians who can't keep their hands off the money?

The only protection that current and future Social Security beneficiaries have is that they cast a lot of votes. However, as politicians continue to hide the true deficits through use of the Social Security trust funds without regard to future needs, confidence in the system will erode, especially among younger workers.

As the ratio of retirees to workers continues to grow, younger workers will face enormous payroll taxes. Some economists say the combined payroll tax would have to reach 27 to 37 percent sometime between the years 2020 and 2030 — a tax rate that, on top of other taxes, would cause the economy to collapse. Others say that estimate is far too high.

But this much is clear: If something is not done to get the federal budget in balance — to stop the trust fund misuse — younger workers will come to the conclusion that there will be no benefits left for them when they retire. Consequently, they will form the first "anti-Social Security" bloc of voters this country has seen since the program was begun by FDR. And those who think Social Security is untouchable will learn only too late how wrong they are.

6.
THE EXPLOSION
OF SPENDING

Through the operation of the Social Security trust funds, politicians have "borrowed" nearly $500 billion. How do they spend the money?

Ever wonder why the federal budget gets bigger and bigger each year? Because spending is like a drug, and the politicians are hooked.

The federal government has spent billions of dollars to bail out corrupt Third World dictatorships, to provide insurance for companies that take jobs overseas, and to do tens of thousands of other wasteful, counterproductive, and foolish things.

Over the past few years, it sometimes seemed that there was nothing on which the folks in Wash-

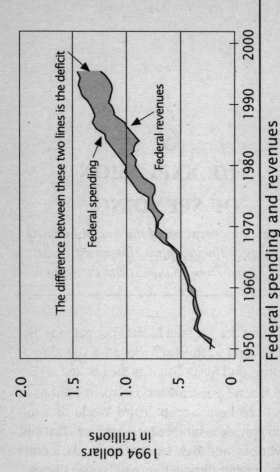

Federal spending and revenues

The difference between these two lines is the deficit

Federal spending

Federal revenues

1994 dollars in trillions

2.0
1.5
1.0
.5
0

1950   1960   1970   1980   1990   2000

This chart shows that -- contrary to the claims of AARP -- budget deficits were not caused by the 1981 Reagan-Kemp-Roth tax cut. Rather, deficits were caused by massive increases in government spending.

ington wouldn't try to spend our hard-earned tax dollars, if they thought it would get them a few votes.

These items appeared in the 1990 budget bill:

- $500,000 to make Lawrence Welk's birthplace a tourist attraction.
- $180 million for the National Endowment for the Arts, which has produced such fine art as a crucifix in a jar of urine and a self-portrait of a photographer with a bullwhip in his behind.
- $6 million for the search for ETs in outer space.
- $10 million for a National Drug Intelligence Center that neither the Pentagon nor the Drug Enforcement Agency wanted.
- $1 million to develop a national policy on bicycling and walking.
- $64 million for the subway system in Washington, D.C. — America's richest city.
- $500,000 for a woodpecker habitat in North Carolina.

Here's how columnist Walter Williams described the 1990 tax hike: Congress and the White House "tell us we need to raise taxes so they can continue funding an unending list of nonsense like $2.1 million to survey American sex habits and attitudes, $700,000 for the Census Bureau to count trees, shrubs, and ornamental flowers, $6.4 million for a Bavarian-style ski resort in Idaho,

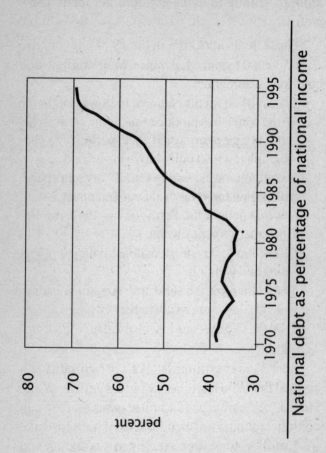

National debt as percentage of national income

$170,000 for a Dunkin Donuts store in Lawton, Ohio, $11 million to construct a harbor for private pleasure boats in Cleveland, and $6 million in handouts for beekeepers."

In 1992, Americans for a Balanced Budget uncovered these examples:

- $320,000 for the purchase of the home of President McKinley's in-laws.
- $5 million for a parliament building in the Solomon Islands.
- $114,000 for an Irish golf video.
- $510,000 for the Teen Gay Pride Fair.
- $18.4 million for the Democratic and Republican conventions.
- $8 million for a religious school in Paris, France.
- $3.75 million for the Poultry Center of Excellence.
- $200,000 for a study on how to commemorate Route 66.

That year, it was revealed that Paul Newman got $50,000 to help him sell his salad dressing overseas. Under the same program, Pillsbury got $1.2 million, Gallo wine got $5 million, and Sunkist got $9.2 million. A group of cattlemen got $394,000 to promote bull semen. And McDonald's got $465,000 to help sell Chicken McNuggets.

In 1993, the U.S.-taxpayer-funded World Bank

approved $458 million in loans to Iran, which the U.S. State Department classifies as a terrorist state.

According to the U.S. Conference of Mayors, President Clinton's proposed "economic stimulus" package that year included:

- $1 million for an indoor baseball field in Huntsville, Alabama.
- $150,000 for picnic shelter repair in Birmingham.
- $3.5 million to renovate a theater in Phoenix.
- $1.3 million for bike paths in Modesto, California.
- $800,000 for research for a bike path in Eugene, Oregon.
- $30,000 for an ice-skating warming hut in Manchester, Connecticut.
- $1 million for a casino building in West Haven, Connecticut.
- $28,000 to resurface tennis courts in Evanston, Illinois.
- $400,000 for carousel renovations in East Providence, Rhode Island.
- $2.5 million to build an alpine slide in Caguas, Puerto Rico.

In 1994, these examples of government spending were uncovered by Citizens Against Government Waste:

- $2 million for the 1996 Summer Olympics.
- $6 million for the World Cup.

- $11.5 million for modernization of the power plant at the Philadelphia Naval Yard, which is set to be closed.
- $40 million for a two-mile streetcar line in Orlando, in an area served by a free shuttle bus.
- $2.4 million for a parking garage for 18 federal employees in Burlington, Iowa.
- $9 million for the National Textile Center.
- $250,000 for the Toledo Farmer's Market.
- $300,000 for construction at the Lake O' The Pines in Texas.

The folks in Washington can't even keep pork out of crime legislation. The 1994 Crime Bill included arts and crafts and dancing programs and Midnight Basketball, and provided for twice as many social workers as police officers.

———

There are those who say that such lists don't really matter, because all the funny examples of pork barrel spending don't add up to much as a percentage of the total budget.

The truth is that for every example that's funny or obviously stupid, there are dozens that are equally foolish but not so obvious.

What these boondoggles and examples of pork prove is that Congress and the White House under both Republican and Democratic presidents have been unwilling to cut even the most ridiculous-sounding examples of spending. If they won't cut government funding of obscene art, for example, what will they cut?

————

Adjusted for inflation and measured in 1994 dollars, annual spending by the federal government passed the $600 billion mark in 1966. It passed the $700 billion mark in 1968, the $800 billion mark in 1972, the $900 billion mark in 1975, and the $1,000 billion ($1 trillion) mark in 1977. It hit $1.1 trillion in 1981, $1.2 trillion in 1983, $1.3 trillion in 1985, and $1.4 trillion in 1990.

Federal spending is now almost $1.5 trillion a year.

During the 1980s, a rapidly growing economy was able to accommodate the increased tax burden. During that period, U.S. economic *growth* was equal to the *entire* economic output of Germany (both east and west). It was equal to two-thirds of the total economic output of Japan. U.S. government revenues, adjusted for inflation, grew by one-third during the decade. Yet, despite the slowdown in military spending that followed victory in the Cold War, government spending grew even faster than the economy's ability to finance it.

President Reagan attempted to rein in the growth of government. His budgets, which had to clear the Democratic-controlled House, were routinely labelled DOA — "dead on arrival" — but he did manage to slow the growth of government spending temporarily. In one year, Fiscal 1987, government spending adjusted for inflation actually fell before resuming its upward climb.

Reagan's effort to control spending wasn't in vain. The federal deficit, as a share of the nation's economy, fell each year during the second Reagan Administration.

During the Bush Administration, however, spending accelerated. The defeat of the Soviet Union was supposed to give American taxpayers a "peace dividend," but Congress and the Bush Administration increased domestic spending by $2 for every $1 that was cut from defense. In all, President Bush increased federal spending 13 times as fast as President Reagan.

In 1993, President Bush bowed to pressure from Congress and agreed to a huge tax increase. The tax increase was supposed to reduce the deficit by $500 billion over five years; instead, it increased the deficit by $700 billion. That $1.2 trillion difference — the difference between a $500 billion cut and a $700 billion increase — was the equivalent of nearly $1,000 per year for each man, woman, and child in the United States.

When President Clinton took office, many Americans were hopeful that he would reverse the massive spending increases and resulting deficits of the Bush years. In his book of campaign promises, *Putting People First*, Clinton had declared: "My [economic] plan will cut the deficit in half within four years, and assure that the deficit continues to fall each year after that."

That promise notwithstanding, government spending continued to skyrocket in the Clinton Administration. By 1994, following the largest tax increase in American history, the Administration was projecting deficits of $200 billion or more year after year — in the common phrase, "as far as the eye can see."

Two weeks before the 1994 election, a secret White House memorandum was leaked to a Republican strategist, who passed it along to the news media. The memo, prepared for President Clinton by his top budget aide, Alice Rivlin, outlined various options for the President to deal with the nation's fiscal problems. The options included tax hikes of over $1 trillion, as well as various changes that Rivlin thought should be considered for Social Security:

• Eliminating COLAs for one year, reducing them by one to two percent a year for five years, or reducing them by 0.5 percent a year permanently.

• Raising the retirement age to 70 by the year 2023.

• Reducing benefits by three percent for newly retired workers, beginning in ten years.

• Taxing an additional $10,000 of Social Security benefits.

• Lowering the threshold for taxing 85 percent of benefits to $25,000 for an individual or $32,000 for a couple.

• Including children's Social Security benefits in parents' taxable income.

The memo, titled "Big Choices," was marked "for handout and retrieval in meeting." It was not to be seen by the public. Administration officials described it as a mere "catalogue" of possible actions that could be taken, but many people were disturbed by the fact that the President's budget director would even be considering such possible tax hikes and changes to Social Security.

Less than two months after the leak of the Rivlin memo, there was another sign that Washington politicians were considering cuts in seniors' benefits. Senators Bob Kerrey of Nebraska and John Danforth of Missouri, co-chairmen of a 32-member commission on entitlements, proposed raising taxes, cutting COLAs for retirees, tripling the Medicare deductible, and means-testing Medicare and veterans' benefits.

Behind all the talk of "Big Choices" and "entitlement reform," there is a recognition that the American people and their elected leaders must decide whether to stop the runaway growth of government spending.

If the government continues to spend every penny it gets its hands on, and then some, there will be little left when the time comes to pay out future Social Security benefits. Long before that dark day, COLA changes would reduce the purchasing power of seniors' benefits. Means-testing would destroy the "social insurance" aspect of seniors' programs, turning them into welfare programs. And seniors, who already pay the highest marginal tax rates of any group in the country, will be forced to pay even more.

7.

THE SPECIAL TAXES

ON SENIORS

Thanks to the Earnings Test and the tax on Social Security benefits, working-class seniors —at least in the short term —pay higher marginal tax rates than millionaires.

Who pays the highest tax on each additional dollar of earnings — (a) Donald Trump, (b) Senator John D. Rockefeller IV, (c) Ross Perot, or (d) a 65-year-old who makes $6 an hour?

If you've encountered the Social Security Earnings Test, you know the correct answer is (d).

The test affects nearly one million retired workers and their families, according to the Social Security Administration. For persons age 62 to 64,

the Earnings Test, in 1995, takes away $1 in So-
cial Security benefits for every $2 earned above
$8,160. For persons age 65 to 69, it takes away
$1 in Social Security benefits for every $3 of earnings above $11,280 a year.

In other words, it is a tax of between 33 and 50
percent on each dollar earned by a senior citizen
above the threshold amount. That's in addition to
all the taxes that younger people have to pay.

All told, almost all working seniors face a tax
rate on additional dollars of earnings of at least 50
percent, and many are in the range of 80 percent.

For a typical senior subject to the Earnings Test,
federal income taxes take about 15 cents of each
additional dollar of income. Payroll taxes take
another 15.3 percent (counting the employer's
share). Seniors must also pay state and local taxes,
which vary widely and which are often along the
line of sales taxes, which fall harder on people
with savings.

Now, it is true that seniors who are hit by the
effects of the Earnings Test receive some compen-
sation in the long run. In some cases, the extra
earnings may result in a re-computation of benefits. In addition, future benefits are increased due
to the Delayed Retirement Credit. But this credit
is 3.5 percent for those reaching age 65 in the
years 1990-91, 4.0 percent for those reaching 65

in 1992-93, 4.5 percent for those reaching 65 in 1994-95, and 5.0 percent for those reaching age 65 in the years 1996-97. To be considered fair by actuaries, it would have to be eight percent — a level it will not reach until the year 2009.

———

Often, two people can examine the same government policy and come to two different conclusions. That is true regarding the Earnings Test.

To some, it is only fair that part of Social Security benefits are delayed or denied to those who continue working. After all, Social Security was supposed to benefit *retired* people, not just people who reach a certain arbitrary age.

On the other hand, critics of the Earnings Test say it perversely discourages seniors from voluntarily continuing to work. They see the Earnings Test as discrimination based on faulty logic — based on the idea that there are only so many jobs to go around, and that every job held by a senior citizen is one less job for a younger person.

As evidence for that opinion, critics point out that one of the goals of the New Deal was to raise wages and farmers' prices by creating artificial shortages.

Corn was plowed under and pigs were killed to raise the price of agricultural products, and various methods were used to reduce the number of workers relative to the number of jobs. There was legislation to require time-and-a-half for overtime after 40 hours a week, and some (such as Senator Hugo Black of Alabama, whom FDR appointed to the Supreme Court) wanted to cut the work week to 30 hours. Unions were allowed to set rules that prohibited non-members from getting jobs in many industries. A stated rationale for the program of Aid to Dependent Children was that widows with children were being forced to go to work outside the home, thus supposedly taking jobs from men; Eleanor Roosevelt expressed the liberals'· hope that one day no married woman would work outside the home.

In the 1932 Democratic platform, one of the "salient domestic remedies" was "the spreading of employment by reduction in the hours of labor," according to Ernest K. Lindley's 1933 book *The Roosevelt Revolution: First Phase*.

Frances Perkins, FDR's secretary of labor and the chairman of the Committee on Economic Security that drew up the Social Security system, wrote that, when Roosevelt was governor of New York, the "solution of unemployment problems" was one of his major activities. Among the recommendations he received for fighting unemployment: "to increase old age assistance in the hope of making it possible for older people to retire and so *reduce the labor market*." [Emphasis added.]

In those days, "many believed that providing retirement benefits would also encourage older workers to leave the labor force, thereby supposedly increasing employment opportunities for younger workers," Aldona Robbins, former senior economist in the Treasury Department's Office of Economic Policy, wrote in 1988.

In that spirit, it makes perfect sense to get older people out of the work force by whatever means necessary. A carrot-and-stick approach was used: bribing seniors to retire by offering them a government pension, and denying them benefits if they continued to work. In the original Social Security Act, benefits were to be withheld completely from persons who engaged in "regular employment." That was changed in 1939, before monthly benefits became payable, to deny benefits to anyone who made $15 per month or more.

Originally, the Earnings Test applied at all ages. Legislation in 1950 changed it so that it would apply only to those under 75. The age limit was reduced to 72 in 1955 and age 70 in 1983.

———

The effect, of course, is to deprive the nation

of some of its most productive workers — the kind of people whose genius and talent, combined with decades of experience, could make America number one in the world.

Incredibly, despite the longer lifespans and improved health of today's seniors compared to half a century earlier, far fewer seniors continue to work. The percentage of males 60 and over in the labor market steadily declined from 65 percent in 1930 to 32 percent in 1980.

A study by the National Center for Policy Analysis (NCPA) found that —

• Among those 65 years old, the retirement rate increased by 40 percent between 1970 and 1985.

• Over the same period, the retirement rate for 70-year-olds increased 20 percent.

• Among those age 60 to 64, the retirement rate doubled in the period 1970-90.

• Among those age 55 to 59, the retirement rate doubled in the period 1975-90.

• By 1990, 83 percent of all men and 92 percent of all women age 65 and over were completely retired, making no direct contribution to the nation's annual output of goods and services.

How our nation is impoverished by forcing seniors into retirement!

Obviously, many seniors choose voluntarily to retire completely. But the historical norm in good times and bad from 1870 to 1930 was for about 65 percent of men age 60 and over to continue working. And most of those who retired did so because of poor health; healthy people usually kept working. Since 1930 the percentage of over-60 males working has declined steadily.

How many seniors choose total retirement only because of monstrous taxes?

Here's how the National Center for Policy Analysis described the situation in 1989:

"Elderly taxpayers now pay a tax rate as high as 48 percent on investment income. They pay a tax rate as high as 16 percent on 'tax-exempt' income. Social Security cost-of-living adjustments are taxed at a rate as high as 80 percent. A 'marriage tax' penalizes elderly married couples as much as $3,000 a year. The elderly pay effective state and local tax rates that are as much as 50 percent higher than the rates paid by younger taxpayers."

The situation has improved somewhat since then, with the easing of the Earnings Test tax from one-half to one-third of income over the limit — though it remains one-half for those under 65. Another change was repeal of the Medicare Catastrophic Coverage tax. But seniors are still hit with taxes far beyond those charged to younger income-earners.

Those who think seniors take jobs away from the young are simply wrong. The truth is that seniors, our most experienced and productive workers, create more jobs than they fill. The NCPA estimates that elimination of the Earnings Test would bring at least 700,000 seniors into the work force and increase the total national income by $15.4 billion, though Social Security Administration actuaries dispute that figure.

In the meantime, the Social Security Administration spends over $200 million a year to administer the Earnings Test, with poor results; 60 percent of overpayments and 45 percent of underpayments result from miscalculations of the test.

According to Senator John McCain of Arizona, "The earnings cap is a relic of a bygone era, when it was the policy of this country to discourage individuals from staying in the workplace after they reached retirement age. Today, many seniors must work to meet even the most basic expenses. A person with no private pension or liquid investments (which are not counted as 'earnings') from his or her working years may have to work in order to cover food, shelter and health care expenses.

"The earnings test effectively prevents our nation's senior citizens from working to pay these costs. The value of a $5-an-hour job, subject to the earnings test, plummets to only $2.20 after taxes."

The Wall Street Journal opposes what it calls the "punitive taxation" of seniors, pointing out that "the Earnings Test sends the message to seniors that their country doesn't want them to work, or that they are fools if they do."

Supporters of the Earnings Test say that it helps the poor by hurting the rich. Attacking a plan to raise the threshold, *The Washington Post* declared that the proposal "is a false front for what would be a major federal gift to elderly people who are relatively well-off. . . . In part because of their voting power, in part because of need, the elderly have stood at the head of the federal line for years."

But contrary to what some people in Washington think, the Earnings Test often hits poorer people the hardest. The wealthiest seniors don't need to earn extra income, so it does not apply to them, and the test only applies to income from earnings.

That means that, if a person made a million dollars a year for ten years before age 65, then retired completely, he or she could collect income from pensions, interest, or stock dividends with no penalty. But if a senior is forced to continue working because he or she was too poor to save much money for retirement, the test applies.

In a *Newsweek* report on the Earnings Test, Melinda Beck noted that a widowed homemaker eligible for $300 a month in benefits would lose $2,000 a year if she took a $16,200-a-year job — while a CEO retired on $150,000 in pension, interest, and stock dividends might get $13,056 in benefits with no penalty.

———

In the 1990 Congress, the repeal bill (Congressman Dennis Hastert's Older Americans Freedom to Work Act) had over 250 co-sponsors, a majority of the House — meaning that it would presumably have passed if there had been a vote on it. But there wasn't a vote on it. Powerful Congressmen blocked the measure from getting to the floor.

Congressman Andy Jacobs of Indiana, who was chairman of the Social Security subcommittee of the House Ways and Means Committee when Democrats controlled Congress, kept the Earnings Test repeal bill stuck in committee because, he said, repeal "would be an enormous windfall for people between 65 and 70 who have enormous incomes, usually from professions and business."

Jacobs refered to this supposed windfall as "golf cart money."

As for President Clinton: During the 1992 campaign, he promised to "lift" the Earnings Test. His spokesmen now say he didn't promise to repeal it, only to raise the level at which it kicks in. The Clinton Administration in fact opposes repeal and supports only a paltry $1,000 hike in the annual threshold amount. Even that proposal is conditional on a tax increase or benefit cut to "offset" the amount of revenue that would supposedly be lost. The Clinton Administration has opposed GOP efforts to do so in fulfillment of the "Contract with America."

———

Other taxes also hit seniors especially hard:

• Because Capital Gains taxes apply to property that increases in value — even if the apparent gain is due to inflation only — many seniors face an incredibly high tax burden for selling stock or real estate. In fact, a typical stock portfolio held from 1975 to 1990 would be subject to an incredible 70 percent tax on the real increase in value.

• As part of the 1983 rescue of Social Security, 50 percent of Social Security benefits were made subject to the income tax after the point at which beneficiaries had income of $25,000 for an individual or $32,000 for a couple. For purposes of this tax, "income" included both tax-free income and half of one's Social Security benefits. About ten percent of Social Security beneficiaries were affected at first, but because the tax threshold was not indexed for inflation it is now paid by about 25 percent. Even seniors who didn't pay the tax were affected by it; many of them cut their working hours or stopped working after a certain point in the year, in order to avoid the tax. As a result, many economists say, the government actually lost revenue from the tax.

In 1993, the Clinton Administration proposed an increase in the percentage taxed, from 50 percent to 85 percent. Congress resisted, and in the final version the 85 percent was applied when income exceeded $34,000 for an individual or $44,000 for a couple. These people were among "the rich" who were targeted by the Clinton tax increase.

In a sense, it is misleading to refer to the Social Security benefits income tax in those terms. Because one can avoid the tax by simply not working, the effective tax is actually on the income one receives other than Social Security benefits. The Social Security benefits income tax is, in effect, a special income tax that applies to seniors.

———

We as a society have got to make a decision: Are we going to continue to punish senior citizens who choose to continue working?

8.
THE MISUSE OF THE TRUST FUNDS: "WHAT PROBLEM?"

Sometimes government officials not only deny that a problem exists, but work to discredit and destroy anyone who seeks to expose it. For years, in the face of threats from some of the nation's highest officials, The Seniors Coalition worked to expose the problems with the trust funds.

Tens of millions of Americans, as they plan for retirement, count on the Social Security system for a substantial part of their future income. After paying their payroll taxes throughout their working years, they expect to receive the benefits that they think they have been promised.

But the fulfillment of those expectations is threatened by a practice that some call a betrayal of the public trust: the misuse of the Social Security trust funds.

Many people still believe that the Social Security taxes they pay go into a special account, perhaps even a separate account for each taxpayer identified by their Social Security "account" number. In fact, every dollar that comes into the Social Security trust fund is used immediately. The "surplus" — the amount that does not go for current benefits and administrative expenses — is "invested" in government securities and the money is used to finance the ongoing operations of the federal government.

The money is spent on necessary government operations and on the boondoggles and pork-barrel projects that have caused a budget deficit each year for a quarter of a century. After current benefits are paid out, excess payroll taxes are used in a manner that makes the budget deficit look smaller than it actually is.

With respect to such "excess" money, Congress and the White House leave non-negotiable bonds — in effect, IOUs. Now, there are very good reasons for not doing other things with the money. Dumping it into the private bond market, for example, could severely disrupt that market. But many Americans plan for retirement based on the idea that the Social Security funds are "socked away," and they need to know the truth.

Not surprisingly, most politicians over the years have assured us the money is safe.

For example, Gwendolyn King, then-Commissioner of Social Security, said in a 1992 speech to the National Press Club that her goal was to "dispel some of the popular myths" about Social Security. "Exploding these myths is my campaign, *especially in this election year*," she said. [Emphasis added.]

She claimed that "this notion that the government has raided the Social Security trust funds" is "an outright falsehood."

In fact, King said, "These funds have been invested in special U.S. obligation bonds, the safest, soundest, most secure vehicle possible. Backed by the full faith and credit of the United States."

Congressman Robert Torricelli of New Jersey said "There is no validity whatsoever to . . . claims" that there is no money in the trust funds. He said, "Social Security is solvent at least for decades," and he urged seniors to "ignore" such claims about the trust funds.

Congresswoman Jolene Unsoeld of Washington said in 1994 that "There is no truth to the charge that Social Security funds are being stolen to fund government deficits . . ." She blamed reports of a trust fund raid on "unscrupulous organizations" who want to scare seniors as "a good way to raise money."

A similar view is often expressed in the news media. For example, the *Erie* (Pennsylvania) *Times News* stated in 1992 that, "According to Congress, the Social Security system is well-managed, well-funded . . ." At that time, the Congressional Budget Office claimed that "Today the Trust Funds are flush with reserves."

The *Boston Globe* reported in 1993 that "Neither President Clinton nor previous US presidents have raided the Social Security Trust Fund, according to the American Association of Retired Persons. According to the terms of the trust, payroll taxes paid into Social Security may not be used for any purpose other than for payment of benefits and never have been."

———

At the beginning of this book we mentioned a May 1992 Congressional hearing about "deceptive" mailing practices aimed at senior citizens. At least, that was the ostensible subject of the hearing. Most of the participants, however, aimed their fire not at people who deceived seniors, but at those who had told them the truth about the trust funds.

The chairman of the Social Security subcommittee, of the House Ways and Means Committee, Congressman Andy Jacobs of Indiana, attacked some seniors' organizations for "instilling fear among Social Security and Medicare beneficiaries by making dire claims that the Social Security trust funds have run out of money." Jacobs called these claims — and letters asking for money to fight the trust fund raid — "unscrupulous practices," "scams," and "instances of fraud." He said one purpose of the hearing was to determine the need "for enacting additional legislation to bring a halt to these fraudulent solicitations."

Congressman J.J. Pickle of Texas read a letter he claimed he received from a woman in West Virginia. The letter supposedly referred to one group's claim that the trust fund money has been spent, and asked "Could this be a scam?" "Yes, it is a scam," Pickle declared. (The letter was widely quoted in the news media. A later investigation showed that the letter — at least the version that was reproduced in the official Congressional report — was a fake.)

Jacobs proposed legislation that, if enacted, would have imposed a fine of up to $100,000 per individual copy of a mass mailing. That would amount to an incredible $100 billion on a typical one million-piece mailing containing such information. He suggested that persons who "swindle against the public" in such a way "be given the opportunity to use some authentic official Government stationery — that of the Bureau of Prisons."

Congressman Earl Hutto of Florida attacked the groups for asking their members for contributions. "This is traumatic. It keeps our senior citizens worried and upset." Hutto called for "prosecutions" of those telling seniors about the trust fund problem.

Congressman Peter J. Visclosky of Indiana ridiculed "the notion" that "Social Security benefits are seriously threatened." Said Visclosky: "I am here to expose what I believe is a con game preying on seniors across the nation. . . . The fact is, Social Security and Medicare benefits are safe. . . [T]heir benefits are safe and will be there tomorrow, just as they were last month."

Visclosky suggested that the government use the laws normally used against drug dealers, whose homes and other property can sometimes be seized. Those laws, he said, should be used against officials of seniors' organizations, to secure "complete forfeiture of all assets involved and have them deposited in the Social Security trust fund."

Larry D. Morey, deputy inspector general at the Department of Health and Human Services, lamented that the law at the time did not apply "to solicitations by organizations that use scare tactics or other inaccurate statements by suggesting that Social Security and/or Medicare are going broke."

Social Security Commissioner King noted at the hearing that "mailings that say 'politicians have "stolen" the trust funds,' or that 'Congress wastes Social Security trust fund money on . . . foreign aid to Jordan . . .' are obviously untrue, and cause unnecessary worry about Social Security's ability to pay benefits."

Commissioner King said that her office had worked with "senior . . . advocacy groups" to stop these "unscrupulous activities." In other words, she was working with some seniors' groups — those that denied the misuse of the trust funds — to attack other seniors' groups.

(Later, officials of the Social Security Administration claimed to have received "hundreds and hundreds and thousands and thousands" of letters from senior citizens "frightened" by pro-taxpayer seniors' organizations such as The Seniors Coalition. But an investigation established that the letters did not exist.)

Interestingly, the hearing witnesses, who were handpicked by the subcommittee, offered no criticism of groups such as the American Association of Retired Persons and the National Council of Senior Citizens, political organizations that together receive more than $150 million a year in taxpayers' funds. Instead, the hearing focused on groups that are funded by voluntary contributions from members, chiefly through direct mail.

Many of the participants in that hearing seem foolish today, though their threats were very real and frightening. Anyone who thinks the Congressmen's behavior was "just politics" has never been threatened with imprisonment for telling the truth.

———

A review of the history of Social Security shows that the trust funds were never intended as trust funds in the usual sense, the sort that collect money that is then held (or prudently invested) on behalf of a specific future beneficiary.

"The plan we advocate amounts to each generation having to pay for the support of the people then living who are old," wrote FDR's Committee on Economic Security, which drew up the Social Security system.

Today we know that Social Security has been

effective, dramatically reducing poverty among older Americans and providing hundreds of millions of people with a substantial degree of retirement security. To a degree that few could have foreseen, Social Security has worked.

Yet, in all fairness, it should be noted that some of the critics of Social Security made some valid points.

From the beginning, some foresaw the danger that the funds raised through the Social Security payroll tax would be used to expand the power and scope of the federal government. Some worried that politicians would raid the cookie jar.

Opponents of Social Security and of FDR were quick to raise that objection. "Conservatives saw the new system as a giant tool for increased federal control," *The Washington Post* reported in 1991. "They feared that the Social Security trust fund would become a slush fund to finance Roosevelt's favorite New Deal projects, free from congressional control.

"Many businesses disliked the prospect of a new payroll tax. And on a purely partisan level, many Republicans saw the system as a Roosevelt scheme to buy votes in the 1936 election with promises of lavish future benefits that ultimately would bankrupt the Treasury," the *Post* noted.

The total accumulated amount of "excess" Social Security funds — the surplus of "contributions" received over benefits paid — was originally projected to reach $47 billion by 1980. Senator Arthur Vandenberg of Michigan charged that Social Security taxes would be used to finance budget deficits. Others expressing similar fears included 1936 GOP presidential candidate Alf Landon, the U.S. Chamber of Commerce, *The New York Times*, and the American Federation of Labor.

That's right: *Even before there were any Social Security trust funds, there was great concern that there would be misuse of the Social Security "surplus."*

But John G. Winant, chairman (and the only Republican member) of the original Social Security Board, called the charges ridiculous, a hobgoblin to frighten the unwary. He said that, after five years or so of experimentation, the system could be adjusted to prevent the creation of such a huge "reserve."

Frances Perkins, chairman of the committee that drafted Social Security, wrote that the system was financially sound — up to a point. Even with benefits going to people who had paid into the system for only part of their working lives — "there would be ample funds to meet all immediate payments out of immediate income. But by any proper actuarial estimate, there would be, in the end, an accumulated deficit. The reserves would not suffice to pay benefits when those now twenty became sixty-five and eligible for retirement."

She added: "From an insurance company's point of view this was impossible; but underlying the whole government system was the credit of the United States. Perhaps in 1980 it would be necessary for the Congress to appropriate to make up a deficit."

Her committee, the Committee on Economic Security, agreed to have a system that would be self-supporting until 1980 or so, and then require a subsidy from general tax revenues, because the accumulated reserves would become depleted; alternatively, it was recommended that government subsidy should begin in about 1965 in order to keep the fund balance from decreasing. Or at least some of them thought they had such an agreement.

"We thought we had agreement on this approach," Perkins wrote. But the secretary of the treasury, whose surrogate had signed on to the plan, "declared his flat opposition to any system which would require a government contribution out of general revenues at any time.

"The alternative appeared to be contributions

in the early stages so large both from workers and employers as to be almost confiscatory."

Roosevelt was adamant. In words that have a special meaning for us today, he rejected an underfunded program: "It is almost dishonest to build up an accumulated deficit for the Congress of the United States to meet in 1980. We can't do that. We can't sell the United States short in 1980 any more than in 1935."

The eventual compromise was that the "reserve" (the amount in government bonds) would be large enough so that, with the government paying itself three percent interest on the "reserve," the interest plus current contributions would be enough to finance the program indefinitely — assuming that benefits would not be increased in the future.

Thus, taxes at first would be small enough not to, in Perkins's words, "paralyze the system and frighten the people and Congress." Social Security Commissioner Arthur Altmeyer noted, "You can trust Congress never to require enormous payments as contributions. They will think of some way out."

Abraham Epstein of the American Association for Old Age Security argued that it would be necessary for the government to subsidize Social Security, but, as Perkins noted, "This issue . . . was rather academic in the light of the United States Government's financial condition at that time. Obviously, *so long as the Government was operating with a large deficit, any Government 'contribution' would be merely a book-keeping entry crediting the social insurance fund, rather than actual cash.*" [Emphasis added.]

Though Roosevelt originally insisted on a system that would be financially sound for many years to come by building up a very large fund, he later accepted a change that moved toward a pay-as-you-go system (which could equally be financially sound, if responsibly planned). Perkins wrote that FDR changed his position because he wanted to raise benefits and to expand the system to include more people. "I don't think he ever realized that [pay-as-you-go] was the exact system he had rejected in at least a modified form when the Committee on Economic Security had reported it to him in 1934," she noted.

Another reason for the change was that the economy, which had just begun to climb up from the Depression, appeared headed back down. The Federal Reserve Board's Index of Industrial Production had gone from 125 in the year 1929 to 58 in 1932. In August 1937 it was at 117, almost back to the pre-Depression level. Then it tumbled until, by May 1938, it was back to 76. As

Frederick Lewis Allen noted in his history *Only Yesterday*: "In nine months [the index] had lost just about two-thirds of the ground gained during all the New Deal years of painful ascent!"

In just a few months, unemployment increased by four million, stock prices fell by 48 percent, and corporate profits dropped by 78 percent.

What happened? Many people blamed Social Security payroll taxes, which kicked in at the beginning of 1937. FDR was trying to balance the budget, and, counting the new payroll taxes, the federal government was actually running a surplus. That strengthened the dollar and increased the value of debts, just as millions of debtors were crawling out of the Depression.

So, from the very beginning of Social Security — before even the first monthly benefits were paid out — its financing method was controversial. The big question was always whether Social Security would be financed as a pay-as-you-go system or as a reserve plan, either partial or full. In other words, should there be tax changes in the future to handle projected outlays, or should the system build up a "reserve" whose interest earnings would be used to assist in paying future benefits?

A bipartisan advisory council was set up to resolve the issue, and it determined (as reported in

December 1938) that Social Security should be funded more nearly on a pay-as-you-go basis. Only a "reasonable contingency reserve" — perhaps one year's benefits — should be maintained.

———

The misconception that Social Security money is locked away in a box somewhere — "set aside for people's retirement," as House Minority Leader Richard Gephardt said recently — has been a key factor in the program's longevity.

Soon after Social Security was created, one of FDR's aides suggested that government auditors were just wasting time keeping track of each individual's "contributions" and retirement "accounts." According to historian Richard E. Neustadt, Roosevelt answered, "That accounting is not useless. That account is not there to determine how much should be paid out and to control what should be paid out. That account is there so that those sons of b——es up on the Hill can't ever abandon this system after I'm gone."

In the 1982 book *A Centenary Remembrance: FDR 1882-1945*, Joseph Alsop called Social Security "now the most prominent individual feature he contributed to the modern political landscape, the law setting up the existing Social Security system. What he requested was a straight insurance system, in fact what the Social Security system is today, with both employees and employers paying the insurance bills.

"The resulting taxes on employees were condemned by many young liberals in Washington on the ground that they were regressive and deflationary. The taxes on the employers were also bitterly resented by the business community, and caused another major business-Roosevelt fissure.

"Roosevelt explained to the young liberals that this was the way it had to be done, if the Social Security system was to be immune to destructive political attack and therefore to be sure to last. And the system was immune, and has lasted until the present, just as Roosevelt predicted. Furthermore, no one supposes that the present actuarial problems will cause the system to be dumped," Alsop wrote.

In the book *Free to Choose*, Milton and Rose Friedman noted that "Social Security was enacted in the 1930s and has been promoted ever since through misleading labeling and deceptive advertising. A private enterprise that engaged in such labeling and advertising would doubtless be severely castigated by the Federal Trade Commission."

Early on, critics of Social Security seized upon its financing as a weakness. In October 1936, employers put slips in pay envelopes warning that "Effective January 1937 we are compelled by a Roosevelt 'New Deal' law to make a 1 percent deduction from your wages and turn it over to the government. . . . You might get your money back, but only if Congress decides to make the appropriation." (That was technically correct. To help get the program past the Supreme Court, drafters put the taxing and spending parts of the Social Security program in separate pieces of legislation.)

The slips advised workers to "Decide before November 3 — election day — whether or not you wish to take these chances" — meaning the risk that Congress might just decide to spend the money the way it wanted, not on old-age pensions.

President Roosevelt responded: "No employer has the right to put his political preferences in the pay envelope. That is coercion, if he tells the whole truth. But this propaganda misrepresents by telling only half the truth. Labor and a fair-minded public must place such tactics in a class with the coercion of the strong-arm squad and the whispering of the planted labor spy. This pay envelope propaganda has one clear objective — to sabotage the Social Security Act. To sabotage that act is to sabotage labor. . . .

"Get these facts straight. The act provides for two kinds of insurance for the worker. . . . The first kind of insurance covers old age. Here the employer contributes one dollar of premium for every dollar of premium contributed by the worker; but both dollars are held by the Government solely for the benefit of the workers in his old age. *In effect we have set up a savings account for the old age of the worker.*" [Emphasis added.]

For year after year until 1977, a government booklet, *Your Social Security*, contained this paragraph:

"The basic idea of social security is a simple one: During working years employees, their employers, and self-employed people pay social security contributions which are pooled into special trust funds. When earnings stop or are reduced because the worker retires, becomes disabled, or dies, monthly cash benefits are paid to replace part of the earnings the family has lost. . . . Nine out of ten working people in the United States are earning protection for themselves and their families under the social security program."

According to Paul Magnusson in a 1988 *Business Week* commentary, "The surplus serves a similar function by deluding people into believing that a pool of retirement money is being set aside. But it exists only on paper, a glorious accounting fiction. It's invested in nonmarketable government securities that pay interest, but that's an accounting fiction, too — both the surplus and its 'income' are spent as soon as they're recorded. Still, today the surplus is loudly heralded, supposedly reassuring prospective retirees that their individual nest eggs are safe. Meanwhile, Congress raids the nest, takes the eggs, and leaves a note."

What happens when those notes come due?

Herbert Hoover wrote in a 1952 memoir that the objective of Social Security "was meritorious. The method of financing of old-age pensions, however, was unsound, as the cash receipts were used to pay current expenses of the government, and government bonds were earmarked for the amount. Consequently, many of those insured under Social Security will have to pay twice, because they will sometime have to put up the money to redeem the bonds." At that point, taxes must be raised, or government spending or Social Security benefits must be cut.

As even the strongest New Dealer might admit, even Herbert Hoover sometimes made a good point. Most Americans today would say that he was wrong to oppose Social Security, but he was right when he noted the program's financing problems over the long run.

As we approach the time in the 21st Century

when Social Security receipts are inadequate to pay current benefits — when taxes must be raised or government spending must be cut — many Washington politicians continue to spend money like there's no tomorrow. If they can't balance the budget now, with Social Security running up hundreds of billions of dollars in "surplus," what will they do when Social Security goes into the red?

The federal government's rising tide of red ink is the greatest threat facing the Social Security system. That's one reason that more and more Americans have come to the conclusion that federal deficits must end.

9.
THE BALANCED BUDGET AMENDMENT: SOCIAL SECURITY'S BEST HOPE?

If government spending continues to run out of control, it will become impossible for the government to meet its obligations under Social Security. To save Social Security, the federal budget must be balanced.

It is an irony among ironies. For years, some of the biggest spenders in Congress had attacked The Seniors Coalition and others for exposing the misuse of the trust funds. Then, when they needed an excuse to vote against the Balanced Budget Amendment, they cited what they called "the raid

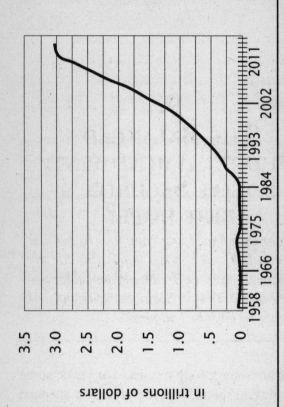

Social Security trust fund money the government "lends" itself.
By the year 2019, it will have accumulated to more than $3 trillion.

on the trust funds" as a danger to the future of Social Security.

Early in 1995, the amendment — considered by many experts the last, best hope to save Social Security — went down to defeat by a margin of one vote in the U. S. Senate.

The tally, before Senate Majority Leader Bob Dole changed his vote for parliamentary reasons, was 66-34. Constitutional amendments require a two-thirds vote for passage.

The measure would have passed had it not been for the dramatic shift of six Democrats who had voted for the amendment in the past. They claimed that they changed their votes because they wanted to protect the Social Security system. This rationale was put forth most forcefully by Senators Kent Conrad and Byron Dorgan, both of North Dakota.

Leading analysts across the political spectrum called the Conrad-Dorgan argument a "fraud," "an outrage," "nonsense," and simply "lying."

Columnist Charles Krauthammer, a former speechwriter for Walter Mondale, declared: "In my 17 years in Washington, this is the single most fraudulent argument I have heard. . . . I mean logically, demonstrably, mathematically fraudulent. . . .

"The best guarantee . . . that there will be Social Security benefits available [in the future] is to reduce the deficit now," Krauthammer wrote. "Yet by killing the Balanced Budget Amendment Conrad-Dorgan destroyed the very mechanism that would force that to happen. . . . Conrad-Dorgan are now posing as the saviors of Social Security from Republican looters. A neat trick. A complete fraud."

Time magazine, in a story by George J. Church and Richard Lacayo, reported: "In opposition, a few Democratic Senators said they were trying to prevent Congress from 'looting' the Social Security trust fund to cover the deficit in other operations. That contention is, to put it mildly, mendacious nonsense. It perpetuates one of the worst myths about Social Security — the idea that the system has piled up vast reserves to pay future pensions. In fact, the so-called trust fund is an empty cookie jar because the Treasury has already raided it for hundreds of billions."

"McLaughlin Group" host John McLaughlin called the Social Security issue a "red herring" designed to divert attention from the real issue, eliminating the deficit. On the same program, Tony Snow said, "What's happened is: Democrats have made a bogus argument. They said, 'We don't want Congress to raid the Social Security trust fund.' Well, hell, they been doing it for 20 years. There's no money left in that fund."

Deborah Orin of the *New York Post* wrote,

"Democrats claimed the measure could jeopardize Social Security. But it wouldn't have changed Social Security's status; it's already used to offset the deficit in Clinton's budget."

ABC's Cokie Roberts, the daughter of two Democratic members of Congress, said, "The Democrats hope that Social Security will work for them as it has in the past. It has always gotten them votes."

———

It's not really fair to blame Democrats as a group for the defeat of the Balanced Budget Amendment. Many Democrats, including Senator Chuck Robb of Virginia and former Senator Paul Tsongas of Massachusetts, backed the measure. Senator Paul Simon of Illinois, former Democratic candidate for president, co-sponsored it.

The Democrats, Republicans, and independents who supported The Balanced Budget Amendement were representing the clearly expressed desires of the American people. By an overwhelming majority, Americans of all ages support the amendment.

In a recent survey commissioned by The Seniors Coalition and conducted by one of the nation's leading polling firms, Americans favor the amendment by 79 percent to 14 percent. Despite

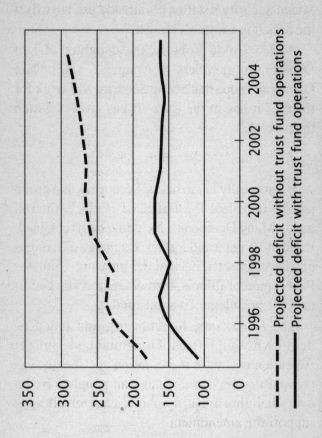

in billions of dollars

- - - - Projected deficit without trust fund operations

───── Projected deficit with trust fund operations

all the scare tactics opponents have raised regarding Social Security and other seniors' programs, Americans age 55-64 favor the amendment by 80 percent to 13 percent and those age 65 or older favor it 71 percent to 17 percent.

People age 65 or older say, by 59 percent to 27 percent, that Democrats in Congress who oppose the amendment are putting politics ahead of the national interest.

Why is support for the amendment so strong among senior citizens? Because they love their children and their grandchildren.

They have no desire to see them drown in a sea of debt.

They have heard about studies showing that today's young people will end up paying more than double the current rate of taxation, unless the federal budget is balanced soon.

They are fed up with politicians in Washington who claim they are for balancing the budget, but whose spending programs are projected to add $200,000,000,000.00 to the national debt every year "as far as the eye can see."

Studies indicate that balancing the budget in the year 2002 and thereafter would cause a 36 percent increase in average income by the year 2021, compared to what would happen if the government debt continued to mount.

There's another reason seniors are for the Balanced Budget Amendment: Because they want to save Social Security.

Every year, the federal government "borrows" money from the Social Security trust funds. This year, it is "borrowing" more than one billion dollars a week. In place of this money, the government leaves IOUs.

Some day soon — some say the year 2013, some say 2019 — those IOUs will come due. At that time, the government will have to pay that money back to the Social Security system. If the national debt continues to grow at the rate of $200 billion per year, it will be virtually impossible for the government to keep its promises to people when they retire.

The misuse of the operations of the Social Security trust funds is happening right now. The only way to stop it is to bring the federal budget into balance. And, unfortunately, we have learned from the experience of the past 20 years that Washington is incapable of controlling its spending without the Balanced Budget Amendment.

"The indisputable fact is that controlling the deficit is the single most important step that Congress can take to protect Social Security," said the amendment's sponsor, Senator Paul Simon of Illinois.

And if the Balanced Budget Amendment exempted Social Security, Congress would simply declare all big-spending programs to be Social Security. (Remember how education and highway spending were included in bills for the "national defense"?) A specific exclusion for Social Security would become the biggest loophole of all time.

Washington had its chance to show that it can control spending without the constraint of the Balanced Budget Amendment. It failed to do so. Now it's up to senior citizens and other Americans to let the politicians know that the people of this country will not tolerate their spendthrift ways.

The future of Social Security, and perhaps the future of our country, hang in the balance.

———

At the height of the debate on the Balanced Budget Amendment, one of the key experts who endorsed the measure was Dr. Robert J. Myers, chairman of the Board of Advisors for The Seniors Coalition. Here is his statement:

For the 37 years that I worked for the Social Security Administration, I strongly supported the program, its goals, and its long-range financial viability. I continue to do all that I can to assure that Social Security continues to fulfill its promises.

The Social Security program is one of the great social successes of this century. It is fully self-sustaining, and is currently running significant excesses of income over outgo. The trust funds will continue to help the elderly for generations to come — so long as the rest of the federal government acts with fiscal prudence. Unfortunately, that is a big "if."

First, over its 58-year lifetime, its budget has, in the aggregate, always been in balance, so that it is not the cause of our horrendous budget deficits and National Debt. At the end of fiscal year 1994, it had an accumulated excess of income over outgo of $423 billion, invested in interest-bearing government bonds.

Second, reducing Social Security outgo alone would not reduce the national debt, but would merely mean that more of it would be held by its trust funds, and less by the general public.

Third, because Social Security is a self-supporting program, reducing its outgo should really result in action to reduce correspondingly its tax income. And, even under the widely-used budget deficit concept, there would be no resulting effect.

Still other people claim that, if the Balanced Budget Amendment were adopted, Social Security benefits would be reduced one way or an-

other in order to meet the requirements thereof.

I agree that, in theory, this could occur. However, on grounds of integrity, logic, and fair play, I strongly doubt that it would ever be done — or even seriously suggested. Certainly, the legislative history should indicate that there was no intention of so doing. In fact, I believe that it would be desirable if a "sense of the Senate" resolution were adopted to this effect.

In my opinion, the most serious threat to Social Security is the federal government's fiscal irresponsibility. If we continue to run federal deficits year after year, and if interest payments continue to rise at an alarming rate, we will face two dangerous possibilities. Either we will raid the trust funds to pay for our current profligacy, or we will print money, dishonestly inflating our way out of indebtedness. Both cases would devastate the real value of the Social Security trust funds.

Regaining control of our fiscal affairs is the most important step that we can take to protect the soundness of the Social Security trust funds. I urge the Congress to make that goal a reality — and to pass the Balanced Budget Amendment without delay.

10.
THE CHALLENGE
FOR SENIORS

Once again, our country must turn to older Americans for leadership in a time of crisis.

In this book, we have shown that, contrary to what the American people have been told, seniors' interests are not protected as a matter of right. The Social Security trust fund money is gone; only the obligation remains, and that obligation can be altered or abolished at any time.

The only thing that protects seniors' interests — the rights and benefits they have earned — is that they can organize, they can support the candidates and causes of their choice, they can educate themselves, they can help other Americans become informed on the issues, and they can vote.

But it's not just their own interests that concern most seniors. They want to make life better for all Americans. They know that if the Big Spenders aren't stopped, it's not just seniors who will suffer; it's their children and grandchildren, too.

As this book is written, our country is entering a new political era.

The New Deal coalition cobbled together by Franklin D. Roosevelt lasted for 60 years, but the 1994 election seems to have brought it to an end. For good or ill, a new set of alliances will dominate national politics. In the years ahead, the tax-and-spend-and-waste politicians who pushed the country to the brink of economic disaster will fight to hold onto power, while the baby boomers, the twenty-somethings, and Generation Xers will continue to seek the right direction for their lives.

One more time, our country will look for leadership to the generation who survived the Depression and won World War II.

America faces tough choices, but there's nothing wrong with this country that a little experience — a little wisdom — cannot fix.

With your help, we can restore fiscal sanity to our national government. We can avoid the economic train wreck toward which we are headed. We can protect the Social Security system from those who would use its resources to gain and hold political power for themselves.

And we can help keep America prosperous and free — for our children, our grandchildren, and all the generations of Americans yet unborn.

APPENDIX.
THE TRUST FUND RAID:
WHAT EXPERTS SAY

In recent years, an increasing number of politicians and commentators have acknowledged the misuse of the Social Security trust funds.

For years, The Seniors Coalition and others who tried to warn seniors about the misleading use of the trust funds were derided as "con men" and "snake oil salesmen."

But what do leading politicians, commentators, and experts say?

• Appearing at a national town meeting sponsored by ABC News, **Ross Perot** said, "Deficit spending is addictive. . . . We've got to put some discipline in the system as opposed to just spending our children's money [and] spending the Social Security Trust Fund money."

• During the second presidential debate of 1992, a questioner who works "in the financial field, counseling retirees," noted that "we funded the Trust Fund with IOUs in the form of Treasury bonds." None of the three presidential candidates challenged that statement.

• During an August 1992 interview with President George Bush, **David Brinkley** of ABC News said that "The [Social Security] Trust Fund consists, increasingly, of IOUs sent over by Congress, which keeps spending the money."

• **Dorcas Hardy**, former commissioner of Social Security told a conference of the Cato Institute that "There are no trust funds, just a bunch of IOUs. That realization comes as a shock.

"Most people still think that there is a savings account with their name and number on it. They believe that the money is stored some place in Baltimore, and when you are ready, you just go and take out your shoe box. When I talk about IOUs," she said, "people say either, 'No, that's not possible,' or 'Well, that's what I thought. I won't get it anyway.'"

• Former Social Security Chief Actuary **A. Haeworth Robertson** wrote: "The government would have us believe that Social Security is accumulating huge trust funds that will be used in the 21st century to help finance the high cost of retirement benefits that will become payable. This simply is not true. Present trust funds, and probably future trust funds, are mere window dressing and have no economic reality."

• The late **J. Peter Grace**, head of the Grace Commission on government waste, noted that "we face a serious crisis within the Social Security Trust Fund which threatens our nation's prosperity and it has very serious implications for anyone who is still working and paying into the system. . . . If you are contributing to Social Security, the thousands of dollars which are supposed to be put away each year for your retirement aren't being put away at all.

"If a private company were to handle your money in the same way Congress is managing your Social Security funds, they would face felony charges, huge fines and long jail terms," Mr. Grace wrote.

• Grace Commission co-chairman **Harry Figgie, Jr.** and University of Arizona Professor **Gerald J. Swanson** wrote in their book *Bankruptcy 1995* (foreword by Senator Warren Rudman) about the "Social Security ruse": " [I]nstead of leaving the money to accumulate in the trust fund, as an individual saves in a retirement account, the government invests the money in its own securities — in effect, lending the surplus to itself. Congress replaces the real dollars that people pay into the Social Security trust fund with specially created, nonmarketable Treasury bonds. These are the federal government's IOUs to itself. Then they spend the actual money they have received.

"Borrowing to meet today's expenses from moneys that we're meant to set aside for the future is a cruel trick."

• **Martin L. Gross**, former editor of *Book Digest* magazine, wrote in *The Government Racket*: "The great unresolved government scandal of our time is the abuse of the Social Security taxes — plus the misuse of that money over the years — by the Congress and the President.

"Today, the abuse has become endemic. In 1992, the government will 'borrow' — a euphemism for 'steal' — $50 billion from the Social Security fund and use it to pay the general bills of its bloated bureaucracy.

"That's not a one-year aberration. It's been going on for some time, and the Social Security fund now has government IOUs for $330 billion. . . . Washington is playing a nasty shell game with the aged citizens' money."

• The late Senator **John Heinz** of Pennsylvania called the raid on the trust funds "embezzlement."

• Senator **Daniel Patrick Moynihan** of New York called it "thievery." He also said, "[We] have now heard the chairman of the Budget Committee not just acknowledge, but assert, that Social Security Trust Funds are being misused. They are being used for inappropriate purposes. They are being diverted to purposes which, in a private trust fund, would be criminal. And so Senators must expect as they vote for expenditures in the months to come — for farm programs, for foreign aid — that they will be asked how much of the expenditure will represent misused Social Security Trust Funds."

On October 9, 1990, Moynihan said: "There are no reserves. They have all been embezzled. They have all been spent."

• Senator **Harry Reid** (D-Nevada) stated on the Senate floor on October 9, 1990: "In the instance of the Social Security Trust Fund, those moneys are used for purposes other than for Social Security recipients, and that is wrong. But here in Congress, we have become pretty careless and callous in what we do with trust fund moneys. . . . The discussion is, are we as a country violating a trust by spending Social Security

Trust Fund moneys for some purpose other than for which they were intended? The obvious answer is yes. . . ." Reid said that "embezzlement, thievery . . . is what we are talking about here." He mockingly called it "the Social Security Slush Fund."

• According to the *Congressional Record*, April 24, 1991, Senator Ernest "Fritz" Hollings of South Carolina said, "The truth is that the Social Security Trust Fund has already been stripped bare. There is no trust and no fund.

"It is a lot like the S&Ls. The savings and loans had a lot of real estate on the books, a lot of property, a lot of shopping centers, a lot of deposits, and everything else, until you looked inside and found out there was nothing there. The assets were strictly on paper. . . . Meanwhile, the Social Security cupboard is bare."

• **Steve Robinson**, an economist at the House Republican Study Committee, notes that, "Contrary to popular belief, the Social Security Trust Fund is nothing more than an accounting device. . . . When individuals pay Social Security taxes, their money goes into the general fund of the U.S. Treasury along with all the other taxes collected by the government. . . . [T]he government currently spends all the taxes it collects, including the surplus Social Security payroll taxes."

• The **Congressional Research Service**'s report for Congress of January 27, 1991, concedes that all of the Trust Funds are used by the government for general purposes and that all Social Security has is a promise by the government to repay the bills: "Perhaps the biggest misconception is that the social security trust funds represent actual resources to be used for future benefit payments, rather than what is in reality a promise by the Government to take steps necessary to secure resources from the economy at that time." Again, that's according to Congress' own research department.

• **Erik Eckholm** of *The New York Times* noted on August 30, 1992: "For now, [Social Security] taxes are far greater than payments. But when the income and payment lines cross — an event now expected in the year 2015 as baby boomers retire en masse — there will be no pot of savings on which to draw. Rather, there will be a pile of IOU's from the Treasury, because the Social Security trust fund is invested in non-marketable Federal securities. The surplus in the trust fund is only a paper one."

• **Steve Mufson** of *The Washington Post* wrote on September 29, 1992: "To keep up the appearance that Social Security is an insurance fund, the bookkeepers at the Office of Management and

Budget say that the money paid into the fund is being 'lent' to the federal government. And about $1 trillion of the federal government's $4 trillion accumulated debt is [owed] to Social Security and other trust funds. But there are no assets — no stock or bond certificates — in the Social Security trust fund; only the government's commitment to make good on the benefits it has promised future retirees.

"Though defaulting on the national debt owed to the public would cause economic chaos world-wide, the federal government can essentially 'default' on part of the debt owed to the Social Security trust fund by cutting back on benefits paid to future retirees. . . . One senior Bush administration official views this as inevitable."

• **Bruce D. Schobel**, a former actuary of the Social Security reform commission (the Greenspan Commission) and former senior adviser for policy at the Social Security Administration, wrote an article entitled "Sooner Than You Think: The Coming Bankruptcy of Social Security" for the Fall 1992 issue of the Heritage Foundation publication *Policy Review*. He noted that the Social Security trustees claim the system is secure. "There is one major problem with the trustees' projection of a 40-year margin of safety, however. There will be no money in those trust funds when it is time to draw them down. The money has already been spent on other government programs."

Schobel explained that "In return for using Social Security's extra revenue, the Treasury issues special U.S. government bonds to the trust funds. At one time, the trust funds purchased marketable securities with their extra revenue, but for many years they have purchased only special-issue bonds sold exclusively to the funds. . . .

"Many responsible observers of the Social Security program recoil in horror at the thought of the Treasury reneging on its obligation to redeem bonds held by the trust funds. They incorrectly compare such an action to government failure to redeem U.S. savings bonds held by individuals. The situation is not analogous. The United States has never defaulted on its publicly held bonds, and is not likely to. The bonds in the Social Security trust funds, however, are not publicly held. They are no more than book-keeping entries, in which one agency of the federal government supposedly owes money to another," according to Schobel.

• Some politicians say the Trust Fund money is "invested," but **David Wessel** of *The Wall Street Journal* explained how the "investment" works. "It's akin to a father putting money into an old cigar box for his young daughter's college education at the beginning of every week, taking it out at the end of the week to pay the light bills, and replacing the cash with his IOUs."

• At a rally on Capitol Hill, May 27, 1993, the oldest freshman Republican member of Congress, **Roscoe Bartlett** of Maryland, declared: "I cannot understand the discussion of Social Security in the context of the budget and budget deficits. This is supposed to be a trust fund. True, it's been raped by the Congress and nothing remains there except IOUs, but it's still supposed to be a trust fund and should have absolutely nothing to do with any discussion about deficits and budget balancing and so forth."

• Senator **Phil Gramm** of Texas said on May 13, 1993: "We have a Social Security Trust Fund, and yet the trust fund buys government debt, frees up resources that the government every day spends on something else."

• The *Houston Chronicle*, in an editorial regarding a proposed "deficit reduction" trust fund, noted: "The president claims the money would be stashed in a so-called special government 'trust fund,' which one top Clinton aide said 'cannot be raided by Congress' or borrowed against as are other federal accounts, including the Social Security Trust Fund."

• **Michael Kinsley**, "From the Left" commentator on CNN's "Crossfire," said, "Look, you know that the Trust Fund thing is a fraud. I'm putting money into it, somebody else is taking money out of it."

• **Jeff Kunerth** of the *Orlando Sentinel* wrote: "The money in the Social Security trust fund — the boomers' retirement bank account — is being borrowed by the federal government to fund other programs and replaced with treasury bonds. Treasury bonds would be a good investment for future retirees if the government were running a budget surplus. It's not."

• On his television program, **Rush Limbaugh** said: "Look at the Social Security Trust Fund. There are countless trust funds out there, and all they do is take the money that builds up and spend it elsewhere. They don't put it on the budget, and a lot of people think that there's a pile of money there, and there isn't. This is nothing more than a ploy."

• **Rob Nelson** and **Jon Cowan**, co-founders of "Lead or Leave," wrote in a *Chicago Tribune* op-ed article: "[T]he surpluses aren't really there. Instead of setting aside the extra $50 billion we collect in Social Security taxes every year, Washington is squandering the money to pay for current government expenses. That money won't be there when we, or our parents, retire. We just have a large stack of IOUs."

• Congressman **John Edward Porter** of Illinois wrote that, "Under previous law, the Social

Security Trust Fund will take in a surplus of $3 trillion in order to offset the baby-boom generation's retirement. However, the Congress has been using this money to finance its irresponsible spending practices and leaving nothing in the Trust Fund but Treasury IOUs. I find this practice both deceitful and abhorrent."

• **Paul Craig Roberts**, former assistant Secretary of the Treasury, wrote in his syndicated column: "To justify an increase in the [Social Security] payroll tax in 1983, the politicians promised not to spend the money or use it for deficit reduction. Instead, it would be put in a 'trust fund' and saved to pay future Social Security benefits.

"In reality, the money was spent as fast as it came in. Today there is nothing in the trust fund except IOUs from the Treasury."

• Clinton economic advisor **Gene Sperling** declared, regarding the proposed "deficit reduction" trust fund, that "This is not like the Social Security Trust Fund. It cannot be raided by Congress."

• *Newsday* reported on the views of **Murray Weidenbaum**, former economic advisor to President Reagan, regarding the proposed "deficit reduction" trust fund: "'Putting money into a trust fund does not guarantee it will be there in the future,' he adds, citing the example of the Social Security and Medicare trust funds, from which

Congress has borrowed money to pay current expenses."

———

And do you remember when President Clinton proposed raising taxes on Social Security benefits? Administration officials called it a benefit cut and said that the money saved would help reduce the federal deficit.

Think about that for a moment. If the Social Security trust funds were in fact separate, segregated funds, money taken from Social Security benefits would have to go back into Social Security and would not reduce the deficit. Thus, the President's proposal *proved* that the funds are being used to falsely reduce the deficit.

———

One last item on the misuse of the trust funds. It shows the cavalier attitude of some self-styled advocates for seniors with regard to the financial health of Social Security.

On ABC News "20/20," correspondent John Stossel noted that "the American Association of Retired Persons, esconced here in its elegant headquarters in Washington, tells people that there is a surplus of money in something called the Social Security Trust Fund. Of course, an accountant would tell you, the money isn't really there."

The broadcast continued:

KAREN MEREDITH, AMERICAN ASSOCIATION OF BOOMERS: "The trust funds are empty. There's not a single penny. The government has not a single penny of reserves anywhere — none, zero, zip."

STOSSEL: "That's a startling statement, but it's true. Every year your FICA payments were mixed in with the government's other revenue and spent that year on defense, the Coast Guard, whatever. There's no money in the trust fund, just IOUs."

HORACE DEETS: "I'm not worried about the security of the Social Security Trust Fund."

STOSSEL: "Horace Deets is executive director of the AARP. [interviewing] You use this word 'trust fund' like it's there. It's not there."

DEETS: "It's not sitting as a bundle of money —"

STOSSEL: "It's just IOUs."

DEETS: "Well, the United States government has an obligation to repay the Social Security Trust Fund for the money it has borrowed."

STOSSEL: "So the United States is going to pay for my kids. And how is it going to get the money?"

DEETS: "The United States is going to have to get its budget act under control."

STOSSEL: "So, what are we going to do?"

DEETS: "Well, if I had that answer, don't you think I would be the leading candidate for president?"

THE ORGANIZATION

Before The Seniors Coalition, there was no organization in Washington representing mainstream, pro-taxpayer senior citizens.

For example, most seniors' groups supported the Medicare Catastrophic Coverage Act. The Seniors Coalition led the fight against it.

Later, The Seniors Coalition worked to inform seniors about the misuse of the Social Security trust funds and, still later, about the dangers posed by the Clinton health care plan, which would have imposed health care rationing on seniors. In 1995, The Seniors Coalition was the nation's largest senior citizens' organization to support the Balanced Budget Amendment.

In 1995, House Speaker Newt Gingrich chose a Seniors Coalition briefing as the forum in which to announce his position on Medicare reform.

THE AUTHOR

Steven J. Allen is a writer based in metropolitan Washington, D.C. He is a graduate of Cumberland School of Law. A former newspaper reporter and radio news director, he has edited political newsletters for senior citizens and served as press secretary to U.S. Senator Jeremiah Denton, then-chairman of the Subcommittee on Aging, Family and Human Services.

He was the only political analyst in Washington to predict the exact number of seats Republicans would gain in the 1994 election.

The Seniors Coalition, Inc. (TSC), incorporated during 1990 in the State of Virginia, is registered with a 501(c)(4) classification from the Internal Revenue Service.

Virginia office: 11166 Main Street, Suite 302, Fairfax, Virginia 22030, (703) 591-0663.

Capitol Hill office: 214 Massachusetts Avenue, NE, Suite 240, Washington, D.C. 20002. **TSC**'s purpose is to heighten public awareness and understanding of the special concerns of senior citizens, and to develop and promote programs dealing with those concerns.

The Seniors Coalition, Inc. is **NOT** affiliated with, endorsed, or funded by any government agency, political party or candidate. Copies of **TSC**'s Annual Report may be obtained by writing to the administrative address listed above or by calling **TSC** directly.

A contribution of $10 entitles you to a one-year membership in **The Seniors Coalition.** Because **TSC** is a lobbying organization, contributions to **TSC** are not deductible for income tax purposes. If, at any time, for any reason, you are dissatisfied with the way **The Seniors Coalition** is representing you in Washington, we will refund your contribution — no questions asked.